Mathematics Education:
A Handbook for Teachers
Volume 2

Edited by

Jim Neyland

Published by
The Wellington College of Education

ISBN 0-908957-10-6

First published in 1995

Published by
The Wellington College of Education
P.O. Box 17-310, Karori
Wellington
New Zealand

Distributed in the United States of America by the

National Council of Teachers of Mathematics
1906 Association Drive
Reston, VA 20191

Printed in the United States of America

Contents

Introduction
Jim Neyland vii

Classroom Teaching
1. The Difficult Road Ahead for the Simple Calculator
    Jane McChesney 2
2. Proof and Refutation
    Jim Neyland 13
3. "I don't know how much to interfere." Independent Group Work
    and Teacher Intervention in the Junior School
    Joanna Higgins 21
4. Eight Approaches to Teaching Mathematics
    Jim Neyland 34
5. The Challenge of Teaching for a Thinking Mathematics Class-
    room
    Bronwen Cowie 49
6. Constructivism in the Mathematics Classroom
    Carol Mayers and Murray Britt 60
7. Making Sense When Learning Mathematics
    Andy Begg 70

Planning, Assessment and Evaluation
8. The Teacher's Influence
    Elaine Mayo 78
9. Planning in Mathematics
    Liz Stone, Geoff Woolford, Kerry Taylor and Ray Wilson 86
10. Assessment of Girls
    Thora Blithe, Megan Clark and Sharleen Forbes 94

Mathematics in Society
11. Innovation and the Mathematics Curriculum: Some Issues from
    the Past
    Roger Openshaw 110
12. Calculating a Square Root before the Electronic Age
    Stan Roberts 122
13. Why Some Mathematics Texts Seem Obscure
    Lindsay Johnston 129

Social Issues

14. Beliefs and Values in Mathematics Education: An Outline of Ernest's Model
    Jim Neyland 139
15. Cultural Issues in NZ Mathematics Education
    Bill Barton 150
16. The Politics of Mathematics Education
    Bill Barton 165

Notes on Contributors 175
Index 177

Contents

Introduction
Jim Neyland vii

Classroom Teaching
1. The Difficult Road Ahead for the Simple Calculator
    Jane McChesney 2
2. Proof and Refutation
    Jim Neyland 13
3. "I don't know how much to interfere." Independent Group Work
    and Teacher Intervention in the Junior School
    Joanna Higgins 21
4. Eight Approaches to Teaching Mathematics
    Jim Neyland 34
5. The Challenge of Teaching for a Thinking Mathematics Class-
    room
    Bronwen Cowie 49
6. Constructivism in the Mathematics Classroom
    Carol Mayers and Murray Britt 60
7. Making Sense When Learning Mathematics
    Andy Begg 70

Planning, Assessment and Evaluation
8. The Teacher's Influence
    Elaine Mayo 78
9. Planning in Mathematics
    Liz Stone, Geoff Woolford, Kerry Taylor and Ray Wilson 86
10. Assessment of Girls
    Thora Blithe, Megan Clark and Sharleen Forbes 94

Mathematics in Society
11. Innovation and the Mathematics Curriculum: Some Issues from
    the Past
    Roger Openshaw 110
12. Calculating a Square Root before the Electronic Age
    Stan Roberts 122
13. Why Some Mathematics Texts Seem Obscure
    Lindsay Johnston 129

Social Issues

14. Beliefs and Values in Mathematics Education: An Outline of
     Ernest's Model
     Jim Neyland 139
15. Cultural Issues in NZ Mathematics Education
     Bill Barton 150
16. The Politics of Mathematics Education
     Bill Barton 165

Notes on Contributors 175
Index 177

Introduction

Jim Neyland

Volume 1 of this book contains a series of articles about mathematics teaching and learning. Volume 2 extends this with further contributions from leading teachers and educators.

When we reflect on our work as mathematics teachers and educators we often use models, metaphors and theories to help clarify our understanding of the teaching-learning situation, and to help guide our future actions. One such metaphor—that of dialogue—although not new, is worthy of renewed interest. In what follows I will briefly describe how many aspects of mathematics teaching and learning, and indeed of mathematical reasoning itself, can be thought of as being like the process of engaging in a conversation or dialogue. But how can this be? What does mathematics teaching and mathematical reasoning have in common with social chatter or simple verbal exchanges of information? In fact, what I am referring to is a particular understanding of the notion of conversation.

So, what is a conversation? It is an interaction between two points of view; an interaction aimed at mutual understanding and the development of this understanding. As a conversation progresses the original points of view change; each reforming in response to the other. It could even be said that a newer perspective begins to emerge, one identifiable with neither of the individual contributing voices, but captured instead in the ebb and flow of the dialogue. In a sense this new perspective could be thought of as residing in the conversational space between the discussants. An attentive observer of a conversation might be able to grasp something of this collective perspective, the product of distinct voices but not specifically owned or articulated by either of them.

A debate is not a conversation because in this situation each party wants to annihilate, rather than incorporate, the perspectives of the other. And neither is a monologue. Here a lone voice speaks; a single line of information or reasoning is presented. Listeners merely receive. They do not interact with, or interrogate, the unfolding viewpoint. You can have a conversation with yourself, so long as you have more than one distinct (internal) voice entering into the exchange. Think, for example, of the instance where you have an important decision to make, and you mentally evaluate the range of alternatives by playing them off against each other.

But what has all this got to do with teaching and learning? It is well known that the 'empty container' or 'blank slate' metaphor for learning is weak both as a guide for practice and as an explanatory theory. There are other images too. For example, we have (i) the image of *training* and *mastery* of mathematical behaviours, (ii) the image of learners progressing from *concrete*, to *symbolic*, to *abstract* representations of mathematical concepts, and (iii) the image of learners engaging in *reflective abstraction* of mathematical structures based on experience with certain kinds of activities.

However, there are problems associated with each of these. Behaviourism has been discredited because it does not result in what we would normally recognise as adequate learning in mathematics, because it fails to deal with student misconceptions, and because it trivialises mathematical knowledge to just those elements which can be taught in a tightly sequenced way. The teaching method based on a progression from concrete, to symbolic, and then to abstract representations is based on a fanciful notion of learning adopted for the convenience of some textbook writers. And reflective abstraction, whilst well supported by research and theory, is still incomplete in two ways. (i) It is based on an individualistic, and purely mental, conception of knowledge construction. It thus marginalises the social dimension of knowledge, and it underrates the importance played by mathematical processes—which are part of the culture of mathematical reasoning—in the structuring of knowledge. (ii) It adopts a conservative stance on knowledge production and underplays the role that critique and evaluation play in knowledge re-creation.

Whilst the image of conversation is also incomplete, it has merit for the following reasons.

(i) It is consistent with the recognition that the learner has a point of view and that it makes sense for the teacher to accommodate or interact with this.

(ii) It admits the possibility that the teacher's mathematical understanding might well be enhanced as a result of dialogue with the student. This ceases to be a possibility if the teacher considers mathematics to be a uniquely structured and hierarchically sequenced body of knowledge, because this is inconsistent with the belief that other structures and processes are both possible and educationally relevant, and that therefore there are always other ways of seeing things.

(iii) It recognises that both the teacher and the student have presuppositions about the purposes and aims of learning mathematics, and that it makes sense to negotiate a common understanding.

(iv) It allows the scope of mathematical knowledge to include, not only concepts and procedures, but those values, attitudes, orientations and processes which make up the culture of mathematical knowledge and which are best learned through dialogue with, and observation of, the carriers of mathematical culture; teachers.

(v) It makes it possible to transcend a purely conservative approach to knowledge production by allowing for a critical interrogation of mathematical knowledge structures, and a critical evaluation of the explicit, and implicit, uses to which these are put. In this context the teacher is more than the carrier of culture; he or she is an agent of cultural renewal.

(vi) It views learning not just as an activity—the sort of learning which occurs quite naturally when one is in a stimulating environment—but as an *action*, a deliberate, intensional act of reasoning and structuring. And here is where the image of conversation is multi-layered, because mathematical reasoning and structuring are also dialogical (conversational) in significant ways.

So, how is mathematical reasoning conversational? There are several ways. The most obvious is expressed succinctly in an Hungarian saying: Mathematicians are people who turn coffee into theorems. This was coined to describe the way some mathematicians go about creating mathematical knowledge; they meet together around a table in a cafe and together investigate new ideas.

Secondly, one of the most useful and powerful forms of mathematical reasoning is based on the triad: conjecture, justification and refutation. Here a conjecture is formed and then examined by two sets of alternating voices: voices which aim at justifying the conjecture; and voices which aim at refuting it. Of course these alternating voices can, and often do, occur within the mind of a single person; but they can also occur in group settings. It is well established that both sets of voices are needed for mathematical reasoning and that it is by this means that conjectures are rejected, transformed, and justified. And, what is even more important, this has been identified as an important component of learning.

Thirdly, the process of constructing a mathematical structure out of a contextual situation also has the back-and-forth characteristics of dialogue. When forming mathematical structures there are usually choices to be made and questions to be answered. Can, and should, a structure be abstracted from this problem? Which variables, operations and relations are most useful in this situation? How do we know? Is any element of the problem diminished by making this particular abstraction? And so on.

Fourthly, having chosen a solution strategy, mathematical structure, or proof method, how do we evaluate our choice? I have seen many instances where students have chosen a plausible (but mistaken) solution strategy and derived a solution perfectly consistent with it. It is no good these students asking, How do we know our solution is right? For these students their solution is correct, given their strategy. It is their strategy which requires examination. They need to ask, instead, How do we know our solution *method* is right? The reasoning used to check the method is more dialogical, than linear and deductive (monological). Does the method work for simpler, or extreme, cases? Were the axioms and assumptions well chosen? Can we find a solution by an alternative strategy? Now, it is important to recognise that this dialogical approach to strategy evaluation can also be applied to methods of proof. Students can be asked to take a proof strategy (e.g., 'proof by mathematical induction') as a *conjecture*. Their task? Find reasons to justify and refute it as a method of proof.

Finally, as mentioned above, the reasoning processes behind the critical evaluation, interrogation and transformation of mathematical knowledge are also dialogical.

The alternative to a dialogical (conversational) approach is a monological one. In the above, I have only alluded to the characteristics of a (less satisfactory) monological approach to teaching, learning and reasoning. You might find it useful to develop this contrasting picture as an exercise.

How can we distinguish a dialogical classroom from a monological one? There are a number of criteria which could be used. Let me mention just one; *choice*. If mathematics is presented as 'one-way mathematics'—one method, one hierarchy, one structure, one algorithm—then there is no point in the students engaging in dialogical activity. Choice is a necessary condition for conversational teaching, learning and reasoning.

To complete this section let me address briefly two questions which can be raised about dialogue as a metaphor. Firstly, is it a withdrawal to monologue if I sometimes just *tell* the students something? From a dialogical perspective it is not necessarily a problem to simply present students with information about rules, algorithms, formulae, procedures, and so on. It might even be a very good idea. How can this be? Within a dialogical setting the presentation of a piece of information does not need to cause a breakdown in action-learning. So, as a rule-of-thumb, if the supply of information results in the *continued investigation of mathematical ideas* then the dialogue is continued, and possibly enhanced. If it does not have this result then maybe the situation has become monological with its attendant risk of passivity and rule memorisation. Some teachers, for example, feel they must shy away from presenting students with algorithms for things like adding fractions, on the grounds that to do this prevents the students from constructing their own algorithms. However, within a dialogical classroom, whilst it is considered important that students structure their own algorithms, the teacher can also present the students with an algorithm, but as a conjecture. The students are then invited to see if it works, and to justify or refute it.

Secondly, what about teachers who lecture to large groups of students, or who teach in distance education? Can these teachers use a dialogical approach? There are several ways, the most straight forward being to use the alternating voices of conjecture, justification and refutation as part of the way the lesson is delivered. For example, when considering the relationship between perimeter and area, a lecturer could pose a conjecture such as: perimeter increases with area. He or she could then outline as series of justifications for this conjecture. And following this switch to the 'voice of refutation' and outline reasons for doubting the conjecture. As a result a new conjecture could be formulated and the process continued. In this way the dialogical approach to mathematical reasoning is modelled in the way the mathematics is presented, thus avoiding the highly sequenced and monological forms of presentation which lecturers and distance educators sometimes feel compelled to use.

* * * * * * * * *

To complete this introduction I will briefly describe a few aspects of the New Zealand mathematics education system, for the benefit of readers from outside of New Zealand. I will limit this to just those aspects which are mentioned, but not described, in the chapters which follow.

The New Zealand mathematics curriculum, *Mathematics in the New Zealand Curriculum* (1992), lists the aims and objectives for mathematics teaching for new entrants (5 year olds) to school leavers (about 18 year olds). The aims and objectives are organised into 6 strands: Mathematical Processes; Number; Measurement; Geometry; Algebra; and Statistics. Each strand is organised into 8 levels; levels 1 to 5 cover the first 10 years of schooling, and levels 6, 7 and 8 cover the remaining 3. The year groups 1 to 13 have, until very recently, been called J1 (i.e., Junior 1), J2, J3, S1 (i.e., Standard 1), S2, S3, S4, F1 (i.e., Form 1), F2, F3, F4, F5, F6 and F7. J1 to S4 make up the Primary School, F1 and F2 the Intermediate School, and F3 to F7 the Secondary School.

A government provided resource, *Beginning School Mathematics* (BSM), is used by many teachers in the junior school and the early standards. This resource has a child centred and activity based flavour, and is organised as a series of modules and cycles.

The F5 year is an important year for students because this is when many of them sit a national examination, *School Certificate* (SC). Some F5 students, usually those who would expect to score poorly in SC, study for the *New Zealand Mathematics Certificate* instead, an internally assessed qualification. F6 students study for the *Sixth Form Certificate*, an internally assessed qualification. F7 students can attempt *University Bursary* (or *University Scholarship* for the higher achievers) in one or both of 'Mathematics with Calculus' and 'Mathematics with Statistics'.

Classroom Teaching

1   The Difficult Road Ahead for the Simple Calculator

Jane McChesney

Discussion

- To what extent do you incorporate calculators into your teaching?
- How has the research about calculator use in the primary school influenced your views about the learning and teaching of mathematics?
- What factors make it difficult for you to make the most of the potential of the calculator?

Introduction

There has been a great deal written about the use of calculators in the primary school and there is also a wide range of published resources available for teachers. Yet many teachers are anxious and tentative about using calculators in their mathematics programmes and there appears to be only a limited commitment to using the calculator to its full potential. In this chapter I will outline some of the difficulties and barriers for teachers in New Zealand primary schools.

I used to believe that I had fully accepted the use of the calculator in school mathematics and I had assumed that calculators were for older children and for secondary schools. It was not until 1990 that I heard about CAN[1] and this was the catalyst for me to completely rethink my views about the use of the calculator in the early primary years. The interim findings from CAN suggested that six and seven year olds were exploring number concepts that we would normally teach to older children (Shuard, Walsh, Goodwin and Worcester,

---

[1]   The CAN project (Calculator Aware Number Curriculum) was a curriculum development project in England and Wales, 1985 to 1989.

1991). I was also interested that the teachers in the project had been explicitly asked *not* to teach the standard algorithms[2] but to encourage the children to develop their own methods of calculation. This innovation was so different from what we were doing in New Zealand at that time that it seemed important to find out more about the CAN children who had used calculators from the age of six. At about the same time, two smaller calculator projects started in Melbourne[3]. The CAN project and the Calculators in Primary Mathematics project have been the major influences on our calculator work with teachers in the Waikato region and this chapter will draw on some of the findings and publications from these projects.

Calculators and the Mathematics Curriculum

Mathematics in the New Zealand Curriculum (Ministry of Education, 1992) gives some direction to teachers about the use of calculators.

Calculators ... are learning tools which students can use to discover and reinforce new ideas. Calculators are powerful tools for helping students to discover numerical facts and patterns, and helping them to make generalisations about, for example, repeated operations. (p14)

The Achievement Aims for the Number strand indicate the importance of a range of approaches to computation.

[Develop] accuracy, efficiency, and confidence in calculating - mentally, on paper, and with a calculator; (p31)

Calculators are explicitly mentioned in the Number and Algebra strands in the Suggested Learning Experiences for Levels 1 to 6. The standard algorithms, however, are not specifically referred to - in fact the only mention of algorithms in the Number strand occurs on p44 "explain satisfactory algorithms for addition, subtraction, and multiplication;" and as a cautionary note to teachers on p33. This signals an increased emphasis on the development of estimation and mental

---

[2] In this article 'standard algorithm' refers to the written methods traditionally taught in school for the four operations, i.e., vertical addition, decomposition for subtraction, vertical multiplication, and short division.

[3] These two projects merged to become the Calculators in Primary Mathematics project.

strategies for calculation and a decreased emphasis on the standard written algorithms. The use of calculators as an exploratory aid for young children is overtly encouraged alongside the acknowledgment of children's own invented methods of calculation.

Calculators in the Classroom

Many primary school teachers have been using calculators in their classrooms for some years. Calculators are commonly used as 'number crunchers' (Groves, 1991) for checking a personal calculation such as a mental or written calculation, or for tedious calculations that are only the means to more interesting problems. Calculator 'games' such as *Zap* and *Guess My Number* are also popular. This approach could be described as *accommodating* the calculator into existing mathematics programmes. Yet research suggests that there are more powerful ways to use calculators; ways which use its full potential to promote learning.

Younger children can use the calculator as a counting machine that "allows counting by any chosen number, from any desired starting point" (Groves, 1991, p4). Calculators give younger children access to decimals and negative numbers. Watching children explore numbers in this way has caused many teachers to question their assumptions about how children develop understanding of number. The calculator also allows more realistic problem solving using 'real' quantities (often measurements) rather than 'artificial' whole numbers. Both the CAN and the CiPM projects found that the use of calculators changed the teachers' expectations about what was possible for children to learn. The project teachers found that they had wrongly assumed that there were ceilings for number knowledge. They discovered that children were able to develop competency and understanding about number to a far greater degree than had previously been expected.

An exciting research question . . . is the extent to which the calculator is *causing* changes in children's development of number concepts or merely *revealing* a state of affairs which has always existed. Some teachers clearly attribute the changes to the presence of the calculator, while [for others the] . . . capabilities must have always been there . . . we just haven't exposed them to enough. The calculator ... tells me that the children are capable of much more than we expected from them. (Groves, 1991, p7)

Teachers also found it significant that the calculator provided a way of teaching mathematics that included more discussion, more problem solving, more shared interactions, both between peers and between children and teacher, and more opportunities for the children to devise their own methods for solving problems. In both projects, teachers found that their teaching styles changed gradually and this caused many of them to rethink their whole approach to teaching mathematics.

Teachers discovered that their planning for mathematics now needed to be much more open ended and that they had to be prepared for unexpected results. When something unexpected happened, teachers had to be ready to share their surprise with the children, to explore with them and to learn alongside them. The teacher became much more of a *participator* and a *motivator*, rather than an instructor. (Shuard et al., 1991).

These research findings raise an important question for teachers. Rather than *accommodating* calculators into our mathematics programmes, how can we use calculators to *transform* the learning and teaching of number in the primary school?

Some calculator experiences for learners that illustrate the potential for mathematical learning

1. Number Rolls. Number Rolls is an interesting investigation developed by teachers and researchers from the Calculators in Primary Mathematics project. Working in pairs or individually, children use the constant or repeat function of the simple calculator to skip count[4]. For example, if the children wanted to count in fives, they would press the keys 5 [+] [=] [=] [=] etc., so that the calculator display would register a sequence of numbers 5, 10, 15, 20, etc. The children record these numbers in a vertical list on a "number roll" (a long narrow roll of paper, such as a used checkout machine roll, that can be rolled up).

Some teachers have found this investigation to be a 'rich mathematical activity' (Ahmed, 1987) for a variety of reasons. For example, in a class where there was a range of knowledge and confidence with numbers, the children could choose which numbers to explore. It was common for children in the same class to be exploring skip counting in twos, fives, tens, twenties, hundreds, and many numbers in between. After working on a number roll with one number, the children can repeat the process with another more challenging number. This activity also encouraged a great deal of prediction and speculation about which number would be next in the sequence, and other useful discussion

---

[4]   For an explanation of how to use the repeating function of a calculator refer to Chapter 7 by Brian Storey in Volume 1 of this book.

occurred between pairs of children. The children's ideas about number patterns led to them becoming more familiar and confident with numbers and the number system. Many teachers agreed that this kind of calculator experience merges the Number and Algebra strands of the mathematics curriculum by emphasising patterns in the number system.

Number Rolls is an example of an investigation that can be sustained over time. It is a practical and organisationally straightforward activity providing a secure routine within which the children can focus on exploring numbers. In our work with teachers we have also used a video[5] that illustrates the important role of the teacher as well as that of the calculator. Part of this video shows a class of young children working on a *Number Rolls* activity and also shows the whole class discussion where children talk about their Number Rolls and reflect on their experiences. Teachers have told us that viewing and discussing this video helped them to visualise the Number Rolls investigation happening in *their* classroom with *their* children and to anticipate and plan for further extensions of the activity.

2. Number Squares. This is an idea from the CAN project.

Put a number inside a square. Then put a number at each corner of the square so that the four 'corner' numbers add up to the number inside the square. (Shuard et al., 1991, p12).

Teachers who used this activity have reported a great deal of success. The children seem to enjoy working on it in either pairs or individually. One teacher who tried this activity with a S3-4 class found that the whole class could work on the same basic activity with the numbers varying in accordance with each learner's needs. Typically, when the children chose the number in the square, they first of all chose numbers that were familiar and accessible; numbers within their 'comfort zone'. After a few examples however, they began to explore numbers that were more challenging for them. This teacher also reported that many children were working in ways that surprised her; for example, using decimals and fractions for the corner numbers. (See Shuard et al., 1991, p22 for more examples of children's explorations.) Teachers have found that, like the Number Rolls activity, Number Squares can be adapted to provide more challenging investigations for learners, for example, by changing the number in the square to a

---

[5] This video is titled *Young Children Using Calculators* from the Calculators in Primary Mathematics project, Deakin University, Melbourne.

decimal or fraction, or by changing the parameters of the task by stipulating that all the four corner numbers must be the same.

Why is this activity so rewarding for learners? Firstly the task is well structured; the use of the number square frees the child from recording more formal, recognised equations so that they can concentrate on the numbers themselves. Our observations of the children suggest that they were using familiar patterns within the number system and also decomposing and recomposing numbers (an important aspect of number sense (Sowder, 1992)). Many of the children used the calculator as a 'support technology' and preferred to use their own mental strategies for most of the calculations. It was common for children to enter the 'number in the square' into the calculator display and then proceed to find the corner numbers in their heads. Other tasks that use informal ways of recording such as 'number caterpillars' and 'number webs', are similarly successful (Lindale, 1991 and PrIME, 1989).

The Role of the Calculator

Often the 'real world' contexts for number are more adult-related and not necessarily of interest to a young child. The two previous investigations (Number Rolls and Number Squares) are not real life contexts but are designed for "active participation in mathematical situations" (Ministry of Education, 1992, p18). If we use a bridge as a metaphor, we could say that calculators provide a bridge to a world of numbers and patterns, out of context as we might see it, but still fascinating and exciting to children. Children have more control over the calculator. They can choose which keys to press and when to cancel and start again. The calculator's speedy and transitory facility may mean that children are more likely to experiment with and investigate numbers and calculation. In short, calculators provide a private and fluid calculating environment for young learners. Working together with calculators promotes a shared cultural experience amongst peers where children can enter a world of number that would otherwise be inaccessible to them, rather like the Mathland that is encouraged by logo (Papert, 1980)[6].

---

[6] The analogy with logo is interesting in terms of curriculum development: calculators may be destined to meet the same fate as logo - i.e., one of the most exciting innovations for children but still very much marginalised in terms of the teaching of mathematics in New Zealand schools.

Calculators and Curriculum Change

Given the overwhelming evidence that appropriate use of calculators can transform the way we teach number in the primary school why are schools and teachers so reluctant to embrace the potential of the calculator? I think there are various factors that are inhibiting curriculum development in this area.

Firstly we need to consider our *own* experiences with calculators. When I ask adults about the ways that they would use a simple calculator most would reply along the following lines. "I use a calculator when I'm doing my tax return." "We use a calculator to work out the phone bill in our flat." "I take a calculator with me to the supermarket so that I don't overspend."

In all of these situations and others (such as in the workplace), calculators are used to replace personal calculation. The CAN Project used a perceptive phrase to describe the essential difference between this and the ways children can use calculators: *Adults use calculators to 'get out of mathematics' while children use calculators 'to get into mathematics'.*[7]

This statement highlights an important issue. Children's experiences with calculators in our classrooms will be fundamentally different from our experiences of calculators (both in our adult lives and in our memories of school mathematics). When we were at school calculations were probably valued as an end in themselves and perhaps we even feel that using a calculator is an illicit form of mathematics. After all it was not that long ago that calculators were not permitted in the School Certificate Mathematics examination.

Many parents appear genuinely to be concerned that calculators will have a harmful effect on their children's learning, and in particular that calculators will make their children lazy or unable to remember the times tables. These concerns are understandable given that parents probably have had the same school experiences as those outlined above. And parents have not had access to the research information available to the mathematics education community.

Parental attitudes can be a formidable barrier to the introduction of calculators and the climate of "Today's Schools" may also be having more effect than previously realised. Decision-making processes in primary schools have altered so that inexperienced people are now influencing the allocation of new mathematics resources. Many

---

[7] From a CAN workshop run by Angela Walsh and Hilary Shuard, Cambridge, April 1990.

teachers have told me about the difficulties they have had convincing their Board of Trustees to budget for the desired number of calculators.

Children's access to calculators is not always equitable between schools. Some schools have asked parents to buy or rent a calculator for their child. Others are not in a position to do this. My observations suggest that the school communities, both urban and rural, that are struggling financially are finding it the most difficult to give priority to the purchase of calculators. Simple calculators are a relatively cheap, durable and low-level technology. They are not as attractive as computers, other technology resources, and sports equipment. Sometimes these more glamorous resources are supplied to schools by commercial groups, but this seldom happens for the humble calculator.

There is also another dimension to the calculator debate. This relates to beliefs that are not often publicly articulated but are strongly held by both parents and teachers. These beliefs relate to our own school experiences of learning about number, and many of these are not happy memories. For example, most of us were taught the four standard algorithms in a way that encouraged us to believe that there is only one correct way to add; that is, using the written vertical addition algorithm. Methods such as this are artifacts of the mathematics curriculum of the time. The 'equal addends' versus 'decomposition' debate for an acceptable algorithm for subtraction is the most recent example of the changing fortunes of these procedures. Another powerful memory for most parents is their learning of the times tables, usually by rote and assessed by speed tests or 'mental'. Some parents may also associate the failure to learn their tables with corporal punishment. Regardless of whether these experiences were particularly happy or satisfying, many parents believe that learning the times tables is a rite of passage within our educational culture and that calculators will harm the child's potential to memorise number facts.

The school curriculum, however, is a conservative social institution. In this context, decisive change, even though based on logical argument and research, is likely to be resisted. Some aspects of school activity are treasured as fundamental: and proposals which appear to devalue these aspects encounter a backlash of personal and political prejudice and something called 'common sense'. (Costello, 1993, p23).

The Role of the Teacher

The importance of the classroom teacher may be the crucial and underestimated factor in the changing role of the calculator in the primary school mathematics curriculum. During the past five years

New Zealand teachers have experienced upheaval and rapid change as a result of an education philosophy now known as "Tomorrow's Schools". A succession of new curriculum statements are being imposed on teachers. At the time of writing, primary teachers are attempting to implement new and draft curricula in a number of subjects and they are also experiencing additional pressures to spend more time on evaluation and assessment. These conditions are hardly conducive to a real transformation within mathematics teaching. Often at times of such rapid change, a teacher's classroom may seem to be the only constant in an increasingly unstable school environment. It is not surprising that teachers are reluctant to implement such a radical change to a major part of their mathematics programme.

There are other factors that may inhibit individual teachers from using calculators in their classrooms. We may be reluctant to put aside familiar teaching materials such as place-value blocks in favour of an unfamiliar technology. We may also feel more comfortable with the direct teaching (or instruction) of concepts and procedures than with a relatively risky environment where children construct knowledge and meaning by interactions with others. We may be concerned about classroom management issues during the process of changing teaching approaches in mathematics. And last but not least, we may feel vulnerable in terms of our own mathematical knowledge particularly when calculators have the potential to take the lid off children's mathematical capabilities.

Future Directions

Teachers in New Zealand have been working hard to change the way they teach mathematics. They are trying to make increased use of problem solving and investigation, communication of mathematical thinking, and varied assessment methods. In fact, the use of the calculator for more autonomous learning can be the most direct way of changing our classroom programme and our attitudes towards teaching mathematics. These changes take time however, and as in most curriculum development, it is more manageable and rewarding when we work together and support each other. The research projects mentioned in this chapter have much to offer schools and teachers who wish to change the way they use calculators in the primary school.

Discussion Questions

1. How can we work together to increase our confidence in using calculators? Which staff development model is most appropriate?
2. What are some things that you have tried in your classroom that you can share with others?
3. Are there any existing resources/activities that you could adapt to be more open-ended by using calculators?
4. What are some of the implications of the increased use of calculators for assessment of mathematical learning?
5. How can schools and parents communicate about the use of calculators and thus enrich the partnership they have in promoting the learning of mathematics?

References

Ahmed, Afzal. (1987). *Better Mathematics*. London: HMSO.

Costello, John. (1993). The Precious Futility Of Arithmetic. *Mathematics In School*. Vol 22, No. 3, p41.

Groves, Susie.(1991). *Calculators As An Agent For Change In The Teaching Of Primary Mathematics: The Victoria College Calculator Project*. Paper Presented at the Annual Conference of AARE, Surfer's Paradise, Nov 1991.

Groves, Susie, Cheeseman, Jill, Allan, Annette and Williams, Margaret. (1992). Calculators In Primary Mathematics - The Calculator Projects Reach Grade 3. In M. Horne and M. Supple (Eds.), *Mathematics: Meeting The Challenge*. Melbourne: Mathematical Association Of Victoria.

Groves, Susie, Cheeseman, Jill, Clarke, Cheryl and Hawkes, Jennie. (1991). Using Calculators With Young Children. In J. O'Reilly and S. Wettenhall (Eds.), *Mathematics: Ideas*. Melbourne: Mathematical Association Of Victoria.

Lindale, Carol. (1991). Calculators And Young Children. *Developmental Network Newsletter*. No. 3, pp7-17.

Lindale, Carol And Biddulph, Fred. (1991). Introducing Calculators To Junior Children. In Begg, Andy et al. (Eds) *Same Papers 1991*. Hamilton: Centre For Science And Mathematics Education Research.

Ministry Of Education. (1992). *Mathematics In The New Zealand Curriculum*. Wellington: Learning Media.

Papert, Seymour. (1980). *Mindstorms*. Brighton: The Harvester Press.

Prime. (1989). *The Second Year of CAN*. Cambridge: Prime.

Shuard, Hilary, Walsh, Angela, Goodwin, Jeffrey and Worcester, Valerie. (1991). *Calculators, Children And Mathematics.* Hemel Hempstead: Simon and Schuster.

Sowder, Judith. (1992). Teaching Computation In Ways That Promote Number Sense. In C.J. Irons (Ed) *Challenging Children To Think When They Compute.* Brisbane: Queensland University Of Technology.

2　Proof and Refutation

Jim Neyland

Discussion

- "All proofs in mathematics involve starting with axioms and then arguing systematically from there to derive the required result." Comment.
- What has refutation got to do with proving things?
- Does inductive reasoning have a place in mathematical thinking?
- "Once a result is proven true in mathematics it will always remain true." Comment.

A Mathematical Encounter

Three people, AP, BT and CM, discuss the following mathematical problem.

Problem:
Find the length of the path made by the centre of a circle as it rolls around the outside of a square.

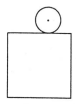

AP:　It seems evident that the shape formed by the centre as it rolls around the square will be a larger square, so we just have to find the length of this larger square . . .

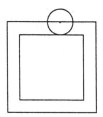

... in fact, the size of each side is equal to the length of the original square plus twice the radius of the circle . . .

BT: Hang on a minute, you're getting ahead of my thinking. It's not immediately clear to me that the shape formed by the centre is in fact a square. Can you convince me we should be examining a square path?

CM: Yes, I'm unsure about that, too. AP, can you justify your claim?

AP: Well, I don't know. What if we make a square and a circle out of card, push a pencil point through the centre of the circle, literally roll the circle round the square, and look at the path made by the pencil? If the pencil marks out a square, would that convince you?

CM: It would only be a special case, but . . . yes I would be convinced.

They carry out this small experiment and decide that, in fact, the shape is not a square but a square with rounded corners.

BT: I've just thought of another way of showing that the shape isn't a square. If it was a square, at some moment the centre of the circle would need to be at the corner of the square. But if this did happen the circle would be too far away from the square it is supposed to be rolling around.

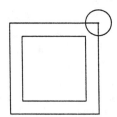

AP: Yes, I suppose you could say that we have now found two ways of refuting the idea that the shape is a square. But this doesn't tell us what the shape actually is.

CM: While you two have been talking I've been playing around with this cardboard example. It seems clear to me that the rounded corners are each a quarter of the original circle, because as the circle pivots around the corner the centre moves through a 90° circular arc with a radius the same as that of the original circle.

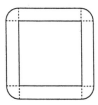

AP: So the length of the path would be the perimeter of the square plus the circumference of the circle.

BT: OK you two. Stand back. I'm going to try and refute that conjecture by seeing if I can place the centre of the circle somewhere on your path in such a way that it doesn't touch the square.

Sometime later, after a period of experimenting . . .

BT: I can't. I accept your theory.

CM: It's a nice result because it doesn't depend on the *actual* square and circle. It's true regardless of which square and circle we are talking about. Let's call it Theorem 1. Theorem 1 says: *When any circle rolls around the outside of any square the length of the path formed by the centre of the circle is equal to the sum of the perimeters of the square and circle.*

BT: And I think we've proved Theorem 1, although we would need to organise our justification into an argument made up of simple, convincing steps.

AP: Before we do that . . . I've just been thinking: Theorem 1 would be true if it was a rectangle and not a square.

BT: Yes, you're right! Our theorem seems to be more powerful than we thought. We can generalise Theorem 1 to Theorem 2 so that the former becomes a special case of the latter.
Theorem 2: *When any circle rolls around the outside of any rectangle the length of the path formed by the centre of the circle is equal to the sum of the perimeters of the rectangle and circle.*

AP: What if we squashed the square to form a rhombus? What would happen then?

CM: Let's draw an accurate diagram and see what it looks like.

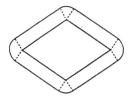

AP: We have circular arcs on each corner, but they are not the quarter circles we had before.

CM: Let's assume that the interior angles of the rhombus are 120°, 60°, 120° and 60°. The dotted lines are at 90° to the sides . . . . so the angles of the circular arcs are 60°, 120°, 60° and 120° . . . . so together they form a circle. So the result still holds!

BT: Now wait a minute. That was for only one particular rhombus. How do we know it works for all rhombuses?

CM: We could repeat what I just did, except use algebra this time. If the interior angles are x, y, x and y, we know that they together make 360°. And the dotted lines are still 90° to the sides. So $2x + 2y = 360°$. So $x + y = 180°$. The circular sector near the angle x must have an angle $180° - x$; but we know that this is the same as y. Doing the same for the other corners leaves us with the sectors having angles y, x, y and x. But we know these add to 360°. So we have our result again.

BT: I bet we can generalise Theorem 2 to include all 4-sided figures.

They try a few more cases of 4-sided figures and state Theorem 3.
Theorem 3: *When any circle rolls around the outside of any 4-sided polygon the length of the path formed by the centre of the circle is equal to the sum of the perimeters of the 4-sided polygon and circle.*

AP: All right! What about a triangle?

They draw a triangle and note, using a special case and then algebra as before, that the sectors still form a full circle.

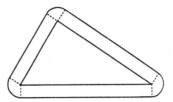

CM: What about a 5-sided figure?

They draw a 5-sided figure and note that the result still holds.

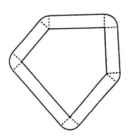

BT: Phew! Can you see where this is heading? Is anyone brave enough to state the Theorem which is looming up fast? . . . . OK, I'll propose the crucial theorem, the theorem which is a generalisation of all the others; it includes all the others as special cases. Theorem 4: *When any circle rolls around the outside of any polygon the length of the path formed by the centre of the circle is equal to the sum of the perimeters of the polygon and circle.*

BT: Let's take a vote. Who thinks it's true?

They all vote 'yes'.

BT: Let's take a rest. I'm exhausted!

Next day.

AP: Shall we try and organise our arguments into a convincing
        proof for Theorem 4?

CM: Well actually, before we do that, first I'd like to try and refute
        it. I'm starting to doubt that it is true.

AP and BT look at CM in disbelief.

CM: You see, if we go back to Theorem 3, I think we neglected to
        look at *all* 4-sided figures. We didn't look at *concave* 4-sided
        figures, that is, ones with corners which go inwards, like an
        arrowhead.

        In fact I think an arrowhead is a counter-example to Theorem
        3 and refutes it.

AP: If you are right, this is devastating news. But why doesn't our
        method work for the arrowhead too? Why isn't it still the sum
        of the two perimeters?

CM: Well, I'm not sure. It just seems to me that there will be a
        smaller path for the arrowhead, because the circle doesn't pivot
        around the concave corner as it did in the other cases we
        looked at . . . it kind of bumps into the adjacent side instead.

BT: Well . . . I don't know. Let's look at a square with a corner
        removed.

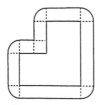

There are five quarter-circular arcs; that's one more than is needed to make the perimeter of the circle. But, the straight line paths at the concave corner are less than the 2 sides of the polygon by twice the radius of the circle. . . Now, does the gain of one quarter arc equal the loss of 2 times the radius? . . . No.

AP: Drat! I didn't want a counter-example to emerge when we were so close to a major theorem. This is really frustrating . . . Hang on! Why don't we change Theorem 4 and eliminate all these irritating concave cases? Theorem 5: *When any circle rolls around the outside of any convex polygon the length of the path formed by the centre of the circle is equal to the sum of the perimeters of the polygon and circle.* Now we still think *that* one is true, don't we?

CM: Very sneaky. I agree you're right, but it seems a bit dishonest and expedient to just keep reducing the scope of the theorem to *exclude* all the counter-examples. Where does this sort of thing stop? Isn't it more intellectually virtuous to face up to the counter-examples and try to form new theorems which *include* them?

BT: I agree with you both. But, I'll bet professional mathematicians do what AP is suggesting. I'll bet they exclude inconvenient counter-examples. Why don't we go both ways: state and prove Theorem 5 and then examine concave cases and see if we can find a powerful new Super-Theorem 6 which includes both the convex and concave situations as special cases?

They examine some special cases of concave angles, including those with right angled corners, and break for the day.

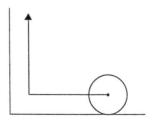

Next day.

CM: Theorem 6 is going to be difficult to crack. I've been looking
        into it and it looks like a description of the length of the path
        in concave cases involves the tan function. And I cannot see a
        way of including both concave and convex cases within one
        overall result.

AP: Well, I've been thinking about it too, and I've got some good
        news and some bad news. I've dreamed up a geometrical
        monster which involves a circle rolling around the outside of
        a polygon but it doesn't fit our previous ideas at all. I have a
        counter-example which suggests that we have been completely
        over-looking a whole class of examples. Up until now we have
        assumed that it doesn't matter how big the circle is in relation
        to the polygon; but it does. What if we have a concave shape
        and a circle which is very large in comparison to it?

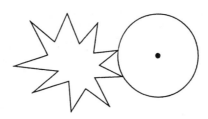

        How are you going to deal with that monster?

BT: Wow! And if we do deal with that monster, how do we know
        there aren't more monsters we just haven't thought about yet?
        Can we ever be certain that we have said the last word on a
        problem like this?

CM: This seems to raise some interesting questions about the nature
        of proof. I mean, can we ever be certain we have actually
        proved something in a situation such as this?

Further Reading

Davis, P and Hersh, R. (1980). *The Mathematical Experience*.
    Birkhauser.
Lakatos, I. (1976). *Proofs and Refutations*. Worral, J and Zahar, E.
    (Eds). Cambridge: Cambridge University Press.

3 "I don't know how much to interfere." Independent Group Work and Teacher Interaction in the Junior School

Joanna Higgins[1]

Introduction

In New Zealand, most teachers of junior primary mathematics organise the children to work, for a large part of the time, on independent tasks in small groups. This chapter explores the role that teachers need to adopt to ensure the success of this independent group work. It examines the dilemmas faced by experienced teachers when trying to make this independent group work more effective, and it looks at the beliefs about learning which interfere with teachers' effective management of groups.

In the New Zealand curriculum, group work is promoted both as a means and as an end. The curriculum emphasises both the active construction of knowledge through discussion, and the process of doing mathematics in collaboration with others. Both the *New Zealand Curriculum Framework* (1993) and *Mathematics in the New Zealand Curriculum* (1992) highlight the importance of group work for promoting the learning of mathematical processes. The curriculum now requires teachers to teach, and assess, strategies and skills for learning mathematics. In the past, children were usually left to discover these for themselves by doing independent activities. Thus the emphasis has shifted from the purely social and organisational aspects of doing an activity together, to also include the mathematical processes which focus on how to do the activity together?

---

[1] This chapter is a condensed version of a paper presented at the American Educational Research Association Annual Meeting, San Francisco, April 1995.

J. Neyland (ed), Mathematics Education: A Handbook for Teachers, Vol.2, 21-33
© *1995 Wellington College of Education: New Zealand*

The Purpose of Independent Groups

Independent groups have traditionally been used to provide maximum peer interaction with minimum adult intervention. A number of studies have noted that there is little interaction between children and teachers during independent work. When intervention by the teacher does occur it is usually focused on social control and not on mathematical processes.

The low level and type of the teacher interaction appears to affect the nature of children's interactions during their independent work. Bennie, Henry and Ratcliff (1990) comment, "This lack of direct teacher control during independent activities gives children opportunity for off-task behaviour . . ." They note "that children were less likely to be on task during independent sessions than class or core sessions", and that "Children are more likely to be on task when interacting with the teacher on maths or maths-related matters". In a more recent New Zealand study Thomas (1994) analysed interaction patterns while 6 to 8 year old children worked independently of the teacher. She found that, to the surprise of the teachers in her study, 91% of interactions were related to the task. This was in contrast to Bennie et al. However, of these, only 38% could be categorized as relating to the cognitive aspects of the task, with 53% relating to the social demands of the task.

The new focus in the curriculum on the processes of group work, as well as the mathematical content, requires a change in the teacher's role. Teachers need to explore ways of providing support for children throughout the group process. Young-Loveridge (1987, p.64) comments that, ". . . children may need to be shown how to use materials in more complex and elaborated ways than are immediately apparent. Therefore, teachers need assistance and practical suggestions about how to do this".

The basis on which teachers group children for mathematics teaching and learning appears to be changing. In New Zealand teachers of junior classes have tended to group children for mathematics on the basis of the content to be covered and the children's stage of learning development (McDonald, Clarke and Kidman, 1991). For New Entrants, grouping is often on a different basis. Most children enter school on the day of their 5th birthday, rather than waiting for the beginning of a term, and thus groups have often been formed according to the date the children start school.

In contrast *Mathematics in the New Zealand Curriculum* can be interpreted as emphasising a more flexible form of grouping aimed at facilitating the learning of mathematical processes. On page 29 it states that students at level one (typically 5-7 year olds) should be "working co-operatively as part of a group by listening attentively, generating ideas, and participating in reflective discussion". Accordingly, many teachers are changing their practice of grouping on the basis of the content to be covered and the stage of learning development, and shifting towards grouping for effective social interaction. However, in a recent study (Higgins, 1994) I showed that teachers are often faced with real dilemmas in determining their role in this new form of group work.

Dilemmas

I don't know how much to interfere.

This is one teacher's role dilemma. The dilemma appears to have arisen from the way in which junior school practice has developed from teachers' interpretations of Piagetian theory and child-centred learning. Choice and autonomy, together with a non-interventionist teacher role, have been seen as being vital for the independent group learning time. There has been a belief that children's understanding of mathematical concepts and their autonomy as learners will be enhanced through the provision of choice from a range of activities or equipment. It is assumed that children will choose the appropriate level of difficulty themselves. This implies a metacognitive skill beyond that of many young children.

Even recent resources such as *Beginning School Mathematics* (1985) have legitimised teachers' use of and belief in this approach. This resource, based on Piagetian theory, includes "core" activities designed to be "teacher-led", and "independent" and "extension" activities which are designed for children, usually in groups, to complete independently of the teacher. The independent and extension activities often take place while the teacher is working with a "core" group. Many of the independent activities are mathematical games which provide a particular context in which children can interact, and provide children with the opportunity to practise the mathematical concepts introduced by the teacher in the "core" lesson. Autonomy is to be developed through the child choosing from among several activities, through determining how the activity is to be done, through deciding where and with whom they work and talk about it, and through deciding how long they spend doing it and whether or not it is completed.

There is a growing awareness amongst teachers that it is not enough just to set children to do a joint activity and assume that mathematical processes will be learned as a result. They are starting to question the common practice of teachers locking themselves into the teacher-led group, and leaving the other groups working independently. There is a move for teachers to experiment with other approaches, for example, by distancing themselves for short periods of time from the teacher-led group and observing the other children working independently. Some government funded teacher development courses have provided guidance to help teachers reflect on their practice and explore a more active role in planning, managing and assessing independent group work. However, this pressure to change the way they use independent groups has created a 'dilemma of practice' (Ball, 1993) for many teachers.

Observation of Independent Group Work
Teachers often expressed frustration at their inability to observe, assess and evaluate independent group work. This could simply be seen as inefficient classroom management arising from their inability to move away from their teaching focus in the "core" group. However it would appear from the teachers' comments in my study that another key reason was that their beliefs about the way children learn mathematics in independent group work create a dilemma of practice about the place of observation of independent group work. After having completed the classroom observations for this study I was frequently asked by the teachers, How did they go? A typical sort of comment was:

I don't get to hear what they're talking about. (Diamond School)[2]

This teacher was surprised that there was not much talk about "other things" when I reported that most of the talk appeared task related. This low level of non task-related talk supports Thomas' (1994) findings mentioned earlier. Another teacher commented:

I don't get a chance to listen to their conversations when they're playing. (Ruby School)

Thus the teachers wanted to know what was happening when the children were working independently at the time they were teaching a

---

[2] The eight schools in the study first reported in *Promoting mathematical processes in the junior classroom* are referred to by the pseudonyms Sapphire, Onyx, Opal, Garnet, Diamond, Emerald, Ruby and Amethyst.

"core" group. On the surface this would appear simply to be a problem for the teacher of not being able to be in two places at once. However, the concern was not as simple as this. As several teachers pointed out, there was a chance that if they were able to observe what was happening during this time their presence could influence the children's behaviour. Their observations would give inaccurate information about the independent learning process.

Well, often the children when I'm around will display behaviour that they think I want. Some children, for instance Georgina, are inclined to say what the teacher wants to hear, hence her remark "I don't like winning games". I'm not sure how reliable their comments might be. They are funny people [5-6 year olds]. (Emerald School)

These teachers were not in a position to judge the effectiveness of the independent work, a major part of the mathematics programme, both because of their belief in a non-interventionist role and because of their use of groups as an organisational device to allow the teacher-led group to function. They are pushed into a difficult situation where they have little information from children's work in groups to make decisions about children's future learning needs.

The Purpose of Independent Group Work and the Related Teacher Role
Most of the teachers in this study believed the main purpose of independent group work was to develop autonomy and independence.

I think a lot of the children, once you talk about independence and talk about it as an idea and show them what you mean by independence, catch on, but a lot of them have not had as much independence. It's a real issue in my mind as I think it's something they really need to have, especially this age. (Ruby School)

However a dilemma can arise for teachers in trying to promote the mathematical processes and concepts for those children who don't display much independence. The teachers know that they must provide structure, but worry about being too teacher directed.

Should I be doing this in relation to them developing independence? Perhaps I'm doing it too often. I don't know. I hope I'm doing the right thing. I'm trying to bring a bit of number into it. (Onyx School)

Their decision about the level of structuring is likely to be influenced by the children with whom they are working.

I have a debate with myself as to whether I'm too teacher directed. I need a programme which is open to challenges. I hope to remove some of the structures when I have these children again next year. (Ruby School)

Some of the teachers treated the social aspects of working together as problems to be solved. The teachers provided a strong framework for social problem solving not just during the mathematics session, but indeed across the school day. The desired outcomes of this problem solving were also made clear to the children. The teacher at Diamond explained her approach.

They seem to sort out - because they know that if I'm with a group then I can't BEAR to be interrupted unless it's "bleeding or death or something". . if something happens I say, well have you talked it over with so and so, no, and if it's a yes then I'll say, well what happened, and then I might have to step in but I'd rather they TRY and worked it out for themselves.

Generally in the classrooms observed there did not seem to be a comparable framework for mathematical problem solving. The mathematical purposes and the desired outcomes of the group activities were often not made clear. For teachers and children these two different types of problem solving, social and mathematical, contributed to a level of overload. This appeared to lead to a conflict between the development of autonomous learning through social problems to be solved and the promotion of mathematical process learning outcomes. The latter appeared to be best fostered by the teacher taking a more active role during the independent learning time.

Given that these groups still had to function without constant teacher attention, one way in which a teacher might take a more active role is in introducing and structuring an activity. However, there appeared to be some confusion about how they should introduce an independent activity (if at all) and when they might do this.

The teacher at Emerald School gave her reasons for deciding to introduce all the activities.

I distinctly remember at training college being told not to give them too many directions but I have the feeling that that's why I thought that maybe I was telling them to do too much in the games. . . I wonder whether or not I have read BSM correctly. I wonder whether I should be giving the children the games and letting them go for it. However I found that when I had a class of 36 and just gave them the games they ended up playing memories, snap and dominoes all the time or sitting and doing nothing. I couldn't bear that so that is why I introduce each activity very carefully. Each teacher-directed time I spend five minutes going over activities as a general rule. The next door J2s work out games for themselves but I doubt that 5-6 year olds could manage this. I can't assume that children know how to play snakes and ladders and dominoes, as they haven't necessarily played them at home, so I really have to start from scratch.

Providing Choice

Teachers face a dilemma when deciding the degree of freedom of choice to provide for children. If children are left to find out for themselves how to do the activity they may not do the activity in a way that brings out the mathematical purpose. Most of the teachers in my study had begun to explore different ways of introducing and structuring the independent sessions. It appeared that a major factor in the success of the teacher's actions was related to the amount and nature of child choice available during this time.

Children's choices are often linked to particular themes, but often these themes are in conflict with the mathematical purpose of the activity. The 'winning' theme is an example. When children can fully choose, and the teacher takes a non-interventionist role, any activity, whether intended as a competitive game or not, has the potential for encompassing the winning theme from the child's perspective. The teachers at both Emerald and Onyx Schools were aware that the children focused on winning in games and described how they tried to steer the children away from this.

There is a thing about winning isn't there. I don't know how you can overcome it - oh well a game's a game and we all had fun I emphasise all the time. Well sometimes they go oh I'm first, I'm second, I'm third - and they quite enjoy that, but then I say well it doesn't matter [if] you're first or second or third - we don't worry about the last but we all enjoyed the game. Give it a positive at the end. The games are fun. (Onyx School)

The teacher at Amethyst School talked about the activities that she had found to be to the children's liking and, arguing from a child-centred perspective, explained how this seemed the most important basis on which to include them in her programme.

When you're introducing them to a game and then you put it in their box you can't really make them do it. You've got to find things that they like working with. They like games, like any cards that can be used for a game of memory. That's competitive of course. I think they're very much focused into who wins in things.

In all the classrooms observed, teachers expressed frustration that despite introducing and modelling an activity children would often adapt it to their favourite style of game. In many cases this meant that the activity was modified by the children to lower the risk.

Yes I've talked to them about it and shown them, you know explained what to do, but they tend to go back and play it like dominoes. (Amethyst School)

The teacher at Emerald School was very aware that some children in her class were not good at challenging themselves.

They were just using the easiest way to do it, not challenging themselves, even those ones that knew - thought they knew - how to do it.

Discussion
What might a teacher do to ensure the success of independent group work in mathematics?
Why might teachers be in a dilemma over their role?
Should any interpretation of an activity, so long as it does not threaten the order of the classroom, be accepted in the name of child-centredness and discovery learning?
What are the dilemmas for the teacher in letting the peer cultural setting of the independent group shape the activity?

The ways that teachers resolve these dilemmas have significant impact on the success of the independent group work. In the next section three extracts illustrate different classroom practices and the mathematical learning in each.

Resolving the Dilemma

When the teacher did not take an active role in setting up the independent group work, the mathematical purpose of the activity was masked by the social demands of the group interaction. When the teacher explained the mathematical purpose of the task, modelled the procedures necessary to carry out the activity, or modelled how to use the associated mathematical language, the students appeared to engage with the mathematics.

In four of the eight classrooms the introductions and feedback were predominantly directive or procedural in nature. In these classrooms there appeared to be a higher incidence of gender based dynamics and peer interaction. These affected the mathematics learning outcomes when children were working independently.

In the other four classrooms the introductions and often the feedback made reference to the mathematical purpose of the activities at least two-thirds of the time. The intended mathematical content of the activities was checked by referring to the stated objectives in the resources from which the activities were drawn. The nature of the teacher's introduction or feedback to the children at the time of the activity gave further evidence of the intended mathematical purpose, and this was confirmed later through interviews with the teacher. Only two teachers frequently gave guidance on how the children should go about a task.

Independent Work which Led to a Masking of the Mathematical Purpose of the Activity
The first extract illustrates the way in which the social demands of the task can mask the mathematical learning. The procedures associated with game playing, such as turn taking, became the focus for these children, allowing the content of the activity to be shaped by the peer culture.

Extract 1
This activity is outlined as follows in the BSM Resource book.

Objectives: Classify objects according to colour or shape. Demonstrate an understanding of the words: same, different, by classifying objects appropriately.
Activity: BSM activity from cycle 2, module 3, Three in a Row. First allow the children the opportunity to match the vehicles on the mastercards. Now teach the game, Three in a Row. Spread the attribute set in the centre of the group. Each child has a mastercard. In turn they throw the dice and place a matching vehicle in the correct position on their mastercard. Sometimes they cannot place one and have to miss a turn. The first player to have three vehicles in a row (horizontally, vertically, or diagonally) is the winner of that game.

John:	I've got 1, 2, 3, 4.
John:	I wish I'd started then I'd win.
Alan:	I think I might win.
John:	You don't really know. Train, train, train, train (puts it on).
Alan:	You've got 5. 1, 2, 3, 4, 5.
John:	1, 2, 3, 4, 5.
Alan:	Yacht.
John:	All got six.
Alan:	A blue car.
John:	Car, car. Yes a train. Where's a train?
John:	Only got two left. Only got two left. Only got two left.
Alan:	Two, four, six, seven (counting the pieces by twos on his card).
John:	No.
	(Alan puts a train on top of a train already on his card.)

John:	No, can't.
John:	It was your turn before. Oh that's what I need.
John:	No.
Alan:	That's all I can do. I've only got two more I have won.
Alan:	I'm going to win.
John:	I've got two more, one, two.
Alan:	One two three.
	(Amanda comes and looks over.)
Amanda:	Why have you got these on top of it?
	(Point to his stack of 3 trains on top of each other.)

Discussion

How have the boys adapted this activity?

Are they likely to meet the aims of the activity? Give reasons.

Suggest a teacher intervention that might have promoted these aims.

Independent Work which Led to Children Engaging with the Mathematics

Extract 2

Extracts 2 and 3 both at Amethyst School show how the same equipment, in this case the pegboards, could be used to promote very different mathematical outcomes. The difference appeared to lie in the structure provided by the teacher for the children to work within. Extract 2 presents an extract from "free choice time" or "maths developmental". Under such circumstances the children are free to choose to use the pegboards for broadly defined mathematical purposes such as making patterns.

Nerida:	I gave you this pink.
Emily:	Hey I just remembered. I'm doing a pattern.
Emily:	If you want to go to Tasha's?
Nerida:	Me?
	She said I could go to her place again.
Emily:	There's so much pinks.
	There's so much pinks [sic].
Nerida:	I'm making a pretty pattern.

Extract 3

The teacher introduced a BSM activity which uses pegboards from cycle 5, module 2, Five in a Row, to a group of girls. This extract shows a very different set of interactions when children were provided with a structure to work within when using the pegboards. It is outlined as follows in the BSM Resource book.

Objective: Demonstrate an understanding of direction and orientation.
Activity: Each child has a pegboard and 20 pegs. The cards are placed in a face-down pack. In turn, the children turn up a card onto a face-up discard pile and put a peg in a matching position on their pegboard (usually a choice of four positions). Sometimes they can't place a peg during their turn because all such positions are already filled. The aim is to be the first to achieve a straight line of 5 pegs. When this occurs, the boards are cleared and a new round begins. When the pack is finished, the discard pile is shuffled and re-used.

Teacher:	Put it down so everyone can check.
	(The children are not saying anything. The teacher models the language for the children: Put it down underneath; Remember you can turn the card around; Which way up is the card? Is that right? Check; Have another look. The teacher continues with the modelling of the language.)
Teacher:	Is that right Sasha?
	(Sasha has put the card away underneath but the wrong way up.)
Teacher:	Your turn Karen.
	Now turn yours around and see if you can make a row.
	Where is that on your pegboard?
	Put that down from the top.
	Count down.
	Put it in.
	Don't wait. Otherwise someone else will have a turn.
	Sasha, you don't just put them away.

The next day Susan, Phyllis and Betty sit down to play the pegboard game, Five in a row. Phyllis and Betty had not done the activity with the teacher the day before.

Susan:	You count up to twenty.
	(Betty counts up to twenty pegs.)
	(The teacher observes that Susan is able to explain the activity to the others and so moves away.)
Susan:	Is that twenty Betty?
	Count them.
	Okay let's match them up to see if I've the same amount as you.
Susan:	Okay Betty, first turn the card over.
	Turn the card around first.
	Turn it down.
	Put it down the bottom.
	You can turn it around if you like.
	Good girl.
Susan:	Turn it over and put it down the bottom.
Betty:	1, 2, 3, 4, 5.

1, 2, 3, 4, 5.
Susan: Your turn Betty.
Betty: I might have to go that way.
                Go that way.
Susan: You can turn the card.
                (Susan looks at it.)
                Oh.
                Good girl. You're already going well.

Conclusion: Managing the Dilemma

The ways in which children work together in independent groups is a key factor affecting the achievement of mathematical processes learning outcomes. The change of practice in independent group work prompted by teacher's interpretations of the new curriculum has, however, created a dilemma for teachers. Better mathematics learning may be more likely if teachers are given the skills to manage their dilemma.

Cobb (1994, p.19) warns of the quest for "an acontextual, one-size-fits-all perspective", and suggests that any perspective should be considered for its "contextual relevance and usefulness" and that we should work towards coordinating perspectives as a way of "making sense of things as we address the situated problems of our practice".

Discussion

1. What dilemmas have you observed in the classroom in relation to child-centred learning and instructional aims? How might these have been managed?
2. Given Paul Cobb's warning that there is not one single answer, suggest ways teachers should manage group work in mathematics.

References

Ball, D. (1993). With an eye on the mathematical horizon: dilemmas of teaching elementary school mathematics. *The Elementary School Journal*, Vol.93, no.4 pp.373-397.

Bennie, N., Henry, E. and Ratcliff, B. (1990). *Beginning School Mathematics. A study of the implementation.* Wellington: Research and Statistics Division, Ministry of Education.

Cobb, P. (1994). Where is mind? Constructivist and sociocultural perspectives on mathematical development. *Educational Researcher*, Vol. 23, No. 7, pp.13-20.

Department of Education. (1985). *Beginning School Mathematics. Introductory Book.* Wellington: Government Print.

Higgins, J. (1994). *Promoting mathematical processes in the junior classroom.* Final report to the Ministry of Education. Wellington College of Education.

Higgins, J. (1995). *Promoting the learning of mathematical processes through independent group work.* Paper presented to the Annual Meeting of the American Educational Research Association, San Francisco, April 1995.

McDonald, G., Clarke, V. and Kidman, J. (1991). *A study of classrooms containing five-year-olds.* Wellington: New Zealand Council for Educational Research.

Ministry of Education (1992). *Mathematics in the New Zealand Curriculum.* Wellington: Learning Media.

Ministry of Education (1993). *New Zealand Curriculum Framework.* Wellington: Learning Media.

Thomas, G. (1994). *Discussion in junior mathematics. Helping one another learn?* Final report to the Ministry of Education. Dunedin College of Education.

Young-Loveridge, J. (1987). *The development of children's number concepts.* University of Canterbury: Education Dept. Research Report No.8.

The author acknowledges the support of the Ministry of Education, Division of Research and Statistics, for this project.

4 Eight Approaches to Teaching Mathematics

Jim Neyland

Introduction

This chapter is an introduction to eight different approaches to teaching mathematics: New Maths, Behaviourist, Structuralist, Formative, Integrated-Environmentalist, Problem Solving, Cultural, and Social Constructivist. This classification of teaching approaches is an adaptation of Keitel's classification (discussed in Howson, Keitel and Kilpatrick (1981), Howson (1983), Bishop (1988), and Ernest (1991)). Keitel identified the first five categories used here; three additional categories have been included. These categories are 'ideal types'; weighted combinations of them can be used as descriptors in real situations.

New Maths

The New Maths approach to teaching was an attempt to radically improve mathematical attainment. It was thought that giving the subject a foundational, conceptual, unity would be a major step towards achieving this goal. Just prior to this time mathematicians had been exploring the way set theory and logic could be used to give mathematics a unifying structure. Accordingly sets, relations, axioms and logic were chosen to build a framework for school mathematics. This was an important new idea in mathematics education: to present mathematics as a coherent, logically organised and consistent body of knowledge.

Unfortunately, although improved achievement was the goal of this movement, pedagogical issues as such were given insufficient attention. For example, the goal of providing logical links between abstract ideas was often achieved at the expense of losing the connections between these abstractions and the contexts within which

J. Neyland (ed), Mathematics Education: A Handbook for Teachers, Vol.2, 34-48
© *1995 Wellington College of Education: New Zealand*

they could be embedded. These connections are unnecessary for the logical development of mathematical systems. However they are important for other reasons, one of which is that they aid the development of the learner's mathematical intuitions.

	Introduction Principle	Uniqueness Principle	Definition Principle
Subtraction	$\forall x \forall y$ $(x - y) + y = x$	$\forall x \forall y \forall z$ if $z + y = x$ then $z = x - y$	$\forall x \forall y$ $x - y = x + {-y}$
Oppositing	$\forall x$ $x + {-x} = 0$	$\forall x \forall z$ if $x + z = 0$ then $z = -x$	$\forall x$ $-x = 0 - x$
Division	$\forall x \forall y {\neq} 0$ $(x \div y) \cdot y = x$	$\forall x \forall y {\neq} 0 \forall z$ if $z \cdot y = x$ then $z = x \div y$	$\forall x \forall y {\neq} 0$ $x \div y = x \cdot /y$
Reciprocating	$\forall x {\neq} 0$ $x \cdot /x = +1$	$\forall x {\neq} 0 \forall z$ if $x \cdot z = +1$ then $z = /x$	$\forall x {\neq} 0$ $/x = +1 \div x$

Example of New Maths from Beberman et al. (1964) cited in Howson et al. (1981)

[Some] opponents of new math criticize it because:
1. It is too abstract and deductive.
2. It is introverted and does not sufficiently emphasize the applications of mathematics.
3. It overemphasises structure, rigor, and symbolism.
4. It includes topics such as sets, logic, inequalities, and number theory which should not be taught in elementary and secondary schools.
5. It overemphasizes relatively new and not very useful areas of mathematics such as topology and symbolic logic and underemphasizes important historical topics such as Euclidean solid geometry, theory of equations and arithmetic skills.

In contrast, some proponents of [new] math praise it because:
1. It illustrates the abstract, deductive nature of modern mathematics.
2. It contains important topics from modern mathematics which have significant applications in other fields of study.
3. It illustrates the unifying structure of mathematics, is rigorous enough to show the sound foundations of modern mathematics and employs appropriate modern mathematical symbolism.
4. It contains topics such as set theory, logic, inequalities, and number theory which should be taught in schools.
5. It includes new and useful areas of mathematics such as topology and logic and de-emphasises outmoded topics such as Euclidean geometry, theory of equations and rote memorization of arithmetic skills.

Bell (1978) discussing New Maths

New Maths was never fully accepted. This, in part, was caused by the abstract nature of the mathematics presented, the emphasis on symbols, the new jargon which accompanied it, and the widespread misunderstanding about what it was all about.

Behaviourist

New Maths had its origins in mathematics. Behaviourism, in contrast, has its origins in educational psychology. This approach draws its basic orientation from the work of a number of theorists including: Thorndike (Associationism), Skinner (Behaviourism), Bloom (Mastery Learning and the Taxonomy), and Gagne (Learning Hierarchies).

Behaviourist approaches were, in part, designed to transform education from a labour intensive to a capital intensive process. The idea had some appeal: carefully organise school mathematics into a precise sequence of small steps in such a way that the learning path will be optimal. The whole programme could then be printed on work cards and mass-produced. Students could work their way through the cards one by one. Fewer teachers would be needed; students would be working at the own pace.

The early proponents of Behaviourist approaches had sound educational goals. They rejected the idea that some people are born to study mathematics and others are not. They believed that a student can learn almost anything, given enough time and the proper prerequisite learning. If the instructional tasks could be arranged into their 'proper' learning sequence, almost all students would eventually be able to accomplish each objective on the chain. Assessment would focus on the mastery of objectives, not on comparisons between students.

Unfortunately, the benefits of these educational goals were overshadowed by the negative side-effects of the means adopted to achieve them, and Behaviourism has been widely condemned by mathematics educators (see for example, Erlwanger (1973), Freudenthal (1978), Ritchie and Carr (1992), Clements and Ellerton (1993), Ellerton and Clements (1994), and Neyland (1995)). Behaviourist techniques do enable the efficient achievement of low order skills, but their use more widely inhibit the learner's intuitive construction of ideas and examination of misconceptions. The focus tends to be on outputs, the end points of learning; on what people can do, rather than on what understandings and meanings have been achieved.

This atomism is the most fashionable wisdom of instruction theory - off-spring of a shallow behaviourism. Behaviourism, too, has long ago left the stage where it studied *behaviour*. 'Behaviour' has been enriched with a plural 'behaviours', which means knacks and tricks, because this is the only thing you can come to grips with; petty behaviours which can exactly be described and measured, rather than global attitude that is obviously 'nebulous'. At present behaviourism is globally identical with the most extreme atomism. All must be divided in diminutive pieces, partitioned, atomised; subject matter must be ground to powder and administered by spoonfuls. It is a demand of the test industry; operational objectives are needed to produce tests. Instruction has to accept the yoke of this philosophy. . . Indeed, atomisation of subject matter is not merely a behaviouristic concern. It is the line of least resistance in technologising instruction. Pedagogues and general didacticians judge mathematics to be their most appropriate victim. Indeed in mathematics you can isolate and enumerate all concepts in order to have them trained systematically one by one . . . as far as you want to go. It is a caricature of mathematics which is quite common. Therefore no subject is as exposed to ruin by atomism as is mathematics. . . But mathematics seems to invite atomisation, and so mathematics is hard to defend. Isolating, enumerating, exactly describing concepts and relations, growing them like cultures *in vitro*, and inoculating them by teaching - it is water to the mill of all people indoctrinated by atomism.

Freudenthal (1978) criticising Behaviourism

The Behaviourist approach can even be seen as anti-mathematical if one sees mathematics as rule challenging, or rule transcending, rather than rule learning. Or if one wishes to present mathematics as a science-like endeavour involving experimenting with mathematical ideas, forming conjectures and attempting to prove or refute them.

In spite the strength of the criticism of Behaviourist approaches, they are still common. Neyland (1995) contains a discussion of the reasons for this.

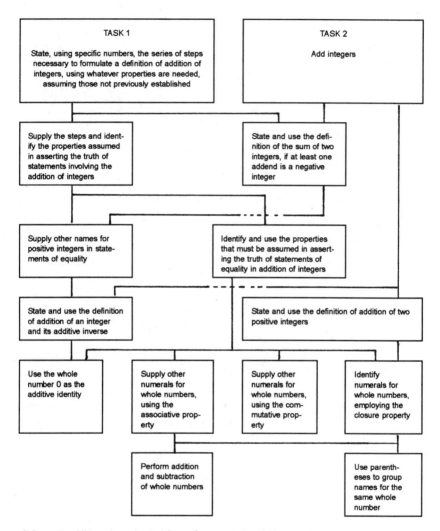

A *Learning Hierarchy*, adapted from Gagne et al. (1962) cited in Resnick et al. (1984)

Structuralist

This approach has origins in both mathematics and psychology. The mathematical focus is based on theories about the structures which underpin mathematics. The psychological focus is based on theories of cognitive development and concept formation. The idea is that if teachers can introduce their students to the essential, underlying, structures and processes within mathematics, these can be used as a framework around which mathematical understanding can be developed. Learning in this way will be optimal.

How is this to be done? The learners explore and 'discover' these structures via a series of embodiments and through a 'spiral' programme which revisits these key mathematical structures in a cycle.

What is an embodiment? It is a concrete, or intuitively accessible, manifestation of the mathematical structure under investigation. For example, Magic Beans embody the key mathematical idea underlying the positive and negative number system.

Magic Beans

Magic beans are of two colours, Red and White. These beans are magic because whenever there is a pair made up of one of each colour, the pair vanishes; they can still be touched, but they are invisible.

A tray contains a large number of beans, with 2 Reds visible. You remove 5 Reds. The result is that 3 Whites are now visible. Explain how this comes about.

If 3 Reds are visible and you remove 2 Whites, what happens?
If 2 Whites are visible and you add 3 Reds, what happens?

Structuralists believe that if students experiment with the Magic Beans they will be learning about the fundamental mathematical structure which underlies the integers. The students would revisit the structure behind the integers via a different embodiment later in the programme, and gradually develop a comprehensive understanding of the essential nature of the integers.

The best known proponent of this approach within mathematics education is Dienes who built on the work of Bruner. This approach can be criticised for sometimes using contrived and even confusing embodiments in the attempt to help students to 'discover' the predetermined structures. It can also be criticised for not putting enough emphasis on students forming their own structures.

Formative

This approach has a basis in developmental psychology and focuses on the natural process of personal development. It is entirely learner-centred and aims to match learning opportunities in mathematics with the learner's natural cognitive abilities. Formativists built on the work of Piaget who emphasised that learners actively construct their own knowledge rather than receive it through their senses ready made. The nature of these constructions depends on the stage of development of the learner's natural thinking structures. Thus a young child will interpret a given observational event differently from the way an older child will. The Formativist teacher aims to help learners develop mathematical concepts in tune with their development in thinking. Accordingly, the emphasis is on evocative learning experiences rather than on the outcomes of learning. For this reason this approach sharply contrasts with Behaviourism.

Our ideas about how to teach arithmetic depend on our understanding of how children learn it. To the extent that we understand how children learn arithmetic, we can try to facilitate their learning. If, however, our theory is wrong, we may even teach in ways that interfere with children's learning. Let us, therefore, examine two different views on this subject.

[One, which is commonly use by resource writers, and about which I am critical, sees learning as] divided into four basic levels, as follows:
1. Concrete level: counting real objects
2. Semiconcrete level: counting objects in pictures
3. Symbolic level: using written numbers
4. Abstract level: generalising number relationships.

This theory is based on empiricist assumptions, according to which all knowledge is acquired by internalization from the environment. . . .

Traditional math educators often say that a number is a property of a set, and that a set of eight objects, for example, has the property of "eight". To me, this is a serious misconception. Sets do not do anything by themselves, such as "have" a property. The action of "having" is done by the child, who constructs number concepts and imposes them on sets. . . . [Thus, I say that] there is no such thing as a number concept at the so-called concrete level . . .

. . . Representation is what children do, and not what the word or picture does. If children have constructed the idea of "eight" . . . they will represent this idea to themselves when presented with the word eight or a picture of eight objects.

. . . [There] is no such thing as a semiconcrete level of learning numbers. . . Once children have constructed the idea of "three" or "eight" . . . they invent their own symbols to represent this logico-mathematical knowledge. . . . [The] so-called symbolic level of written numerals . . . is, therefore, not a level that grows out of the so-called semiconcrete level of pictures.

. . . [The] child constructs numerical relationships through constructive abstraction, and not by going through the semiconcrete or symbolic level.

Kamii (1989) promoting Piagetian ideas and criticising the 'traditional' view.

Because this approach is based on the learner's idiosyncratic structuring of knowledge and not on the revelation of the essential structures of mathematics, it requires the teacher to take an active role in helping each student make sensible connections linking their ideas. Where the teacher cannot provide such individual attention there is the risk that the learning can become unfocused and the whole process can degenerate into a series of unrelated activities.

Integrated-Environmentalist

This approach is based on the view that mathematical knowledge cannot be separated from the contexts from which it is extracted and from which it achieves its meaning. Mathematics is seen as being integrated with other areas of knowledge, subject barriers are down-played, and knowledge is thought of as an integrated web. The learner's environment is used as a source of inspiration and meaning, and as the base for the abstraction process. Teachers using this approach commonly rely on mathematical modelling, statistics, thematic units, and project work, in an attempt to develop mathematical ideas in context. Mathematics is seen as a strand of concepts which can be discovered by exploring problems in the environment. It is also seen as a way of imposing an abstract structure on a contextual situation and reinterpreting the situation in this light. Because the emphasis is on the individual learner constructing concepts from contexts familiar to them, the approach has many of the difficulties associated with the Formative approach.

Baby in the Car

"I parked my car in the supermarket park. I wasn't going to be too long in the shop so I left the baby asleep in the car. It took me a little longer than I had expected, and when I returned to my car I found someone smashing the window with a hammer. 'Stop, thief!' I cried. But the person replied, 'I am not trying to steal your car, I am trying to save your baby's life! Never leave a baby in a car like this on a warm day. Babies heat up much faster than adults.' I thanked my rescuer for saving my baby's life and drove home shaken but wiser."

Do babies heat up faster than adults? Why? Fully justify your claims.
Do they also cool down faster? What are the implications of this?

An example of an Integrated-Environmentalist Modelling Activity

Problem Solving

This approach became a focus for attention during the early 1980s when, in the USA, the National Council of Teachers of Mathematics published the *Agenda for Action* (1980) which called for problem solving to become the basis for all learning of mathematics. In the UK the Cockcroft Report, *Mathematics Counts* (1982), followed suit and called for problem solving and investigation to be included in all mathematics teaching. Problem solving, it was believed, would achieve several educational goals. It places an emphasis on mathematical *processes* as well as the mathematical *content* emphasised by other approaches. Problem solving presents mathematics in context and provides a reason for doing mathematics; to solve problems. Problem solving emphasises *strategies* rather than *rules*. It allows a range of solution methods to problems, and so students learn that mathematics is not just the use of fixed and predetermined rules. Problem solving was seen to be similar to what practising mathematicians actually do. Thus, using problem solving, students get a taste for the creative, developmental, aspects of mathematics. Teachers used the work of Polya (1945) as a source of problem solving and investigational strategies and heuristics .

[The] mathematics curriculum should include numerous and varied experiences with problem solving as a method of inquiry and application so that students can
- use problem solving approaches to invent and understand mathematical content;
- formulate problems from situations within and outside mathematics;
- develop and apply a variety of strategies to solve problems, with emphasis on multistep and nonroutine problems;
- verify and interpret results with respect to the original problem situation;
- generalise solutions and strategies to new problem situations;
- acquire confidence in using mathematics meaningfully.

Curriculum and Evaluation Standards for School Mathematics (1989)

Problem Solving in the School Curriculum

The Problem Solving approach uses problem solving strategies, such as, 'solve a simpler problem first', 'work backwards', and 'try extreme cases' as key processes within mathematics; in fact, ones that make many of the rules taught in other approaches redundant. Mathematics is viewed as an area of knowledge to be explored using these generic strategies; content becomes a context within which the problem solving processes are developed.

Problem Solving Strategies

• Guess and Check	• Make a Model
• Make a list or Table	• Draw a Picture
• Look for a Pattern	• Try a Simpler Problem First
• Work Backwards	• Use Symmetry

This approach has much to recommend it. The focus on using

problems in context enables students to ground their mathematics in something meaningful to them. Encouraging students to find their own solution strategies is empowering; they learn that mathematics is something they can explore using methods of their own choosing. The opportunity it provides for students to investigate new ideas gives them a taste for *making* knowledge rather than just *receiving* it.

The approach has difficulties associated with it. While Problem Solving emphasises the processes of doing mathematics, it is not clear exactly how content knowledge is to be dealt with. This latter difficulty has led many teachers to treat problem solving as a stand-alone unit alongside other content units. It should be noted, too, that some texts present problem solving in a style reminiscent of Behaviourism. This is inconsistent with the aims of the Problem Solving approach which, by contrast, emphasises generic strategies rather than rules, and involves counter-hierarchical elements (for example, the fact that there are many ways of solving problems).

Cultural

This category is not reflected in typical classroom practice. It represents the educational aims of the small group of teachers who work with indigenous peoples. Some groups are asserting their cultural identity and seeking to improve the achievement of their members by establishing firm links between their culture and mathematics. The Cultural approach is based on the belief that all cultural groups engage in activities which exhibit mathematical elements. Western mathematics, now itself a highly developed and explicit cultural activity (enriched by a number of cultural traditions) is also the result of general cultural activities.

Thus the Cultural approach views mathematics as a social and cultural product based on certain activities. It is primarily focused on linking mathematics with the lives and culture of the learner's concerned. It is not essential that one particular set of activities be universal for all cultures. What is important is that the activities reflect mathematical thinking, and be harmonious with the cultural context concerned.

Bishop (1988) suggests six groups of activities: counting, locating, measuring, designing, playing, and explaining. A particular cultural group identifies the ways it uses these activities to develop concepts and ideas which have mathematical elements. These are used as the origins from which more explicitly mathematical ideas are developed, and eventually the process is extended to encompass traditional mathematics. Thus, for example, the cultural activities of 'locating' and 'designing' would eventually include much of what we usually think of as geometry.

This approach has much to recommend it. The learning is context based and grounded in the cultural practices most familiar to the students. It recognises as valid, mathematical activities which might otherwise have been disregarded by the dominant culture. The emphasis on mathematics as a cultural product is empowering, reduces the mystery many associate with mathematics, and gives traditional school mathematics a useful base upon which to build. The grounding of mathematics in cultural activities, instead of the traditional content topics, reinforces the arbitrary nature of traditional mathematical structures.

The approach has many difficulties associated with it. The whole curriculum has to be redesigned from scratch. The teachers need to be very confident and secure with their own mathematical knowledge in order to transform it into a new structure, and they need to be very familiar with the cultural practices of the group concerned.

This whole approach assumes that it is desirable to teach Western mathematics using traditional cultural activities as a conceptual and motivational aid. Some would reject this assumption claiming it is an artificial imposition of an alien interpretation on their traditional activities.

Playing

Playing may seem initially to be a rather strange activity to include in a collection of activities relevant to the development of mathematical ideas, until one realises just how many games have mathematical connections. . . . .   Clearly playing is a form of social activity which is different in character from any other kind of social intercourse which has been mentioned so far - playing takes place in the context of a game, and people become players. The real/not real boundary is well established and players can *only* play with other players if everyone agrees not to behave 'normally'. . . .   Could these characteristics be at the root of hypothetical thinking? Could playing represent the first stage of distancing oneself from reality in order to reflect on and perhaps to imagine modifying that reality? . . . .   [The] quality of the form developed in play can become valued for its own sake. . . . .

Once the play-form itself becomes the focus, and a 'game' develops, then the rules, procedures, tasks and criteria become formalised and ritualised. They are also products of 'playing'. Games are often valued by mathematicians because of their rule-governed behaviour which it is said, is like mathematics itself. I think that it is not too difficult to imagine how the rule-governed criteria of mathematics have developed from the pleasures and satisfactions of rule-governed behaviour in games.

Bishop (1988) discussing the cultural activity Playing.

Social Constructivist

The principal focus of this approach is the belief that mathematical knowledge is socially constructed and validated, and that classroom teaching should reflect this. Social Constructivism has, as a secondary focus, the belief that education in general, and mathematics teaching in particular, should be aimed at encouraging students to see the future as something they can have a part in creating. Thirdly, the approach takes an evaluative orientation towards the uses, and the place, of mathematics in society.

So what does it mean to say that mathematical knowledge is socially constructed and validated? Mathematics is seen as a part of human culture; it is a social, cultural and historical entity. Mathematics develops as a result of a range of human activities and the discourse these generate. To be engaged in mathematical activity is to partake in the culture of mathematising. The things which are accepted as making sense in mathematics are those which can be justified in relation to empirical evidence, those which seem to work in practice, those which result from inductive reasoning and which are resistant to falsification, those which have a high probability of being true, and those which can be formally proven. The last of these are given the status of mathematical 'truths'.

How does mathematics teaching reflect this? Learning is seen not just as individuals forming mathematical concepts, but as the learners becoming involved in a community discourse. The students are seen as a fledgling community who are becoming enculturated (Bishop, 1988; and Schoenfeld, 1992) or socialised (Resnick, 1989) by the teacher into the mathematising culture. Learning is seen from a Vygotskian perspective; one which emphasises the social dimension of knowledge. Teaching focuses on classroom discourse in the context of relevant mathematical investigations, problems and tasks, with the teacher, the agent of enculturation, playing a key role.

The Social Constructivist approach aims to empower students to contribute to the reconstruction (as distinct from reproduction) of society and the world. Thus students are encouraged to form new understandings of mathematics (ones appropriate for the new age) using their interpretations of the existing ones as part of their reference frame. In a similar way, mathematics is presented as a problem solving tool which can contribute to the solution of more general problems posed by students.

The Barefoot Statistician

Evans (1986) describes the barefoot statistician. The barefoot statistician is the mathematical equivalent of the barefoot doctor in China. The barefoot doctors were community based health workers, from among the people, educated to promote community health and give health care in cases involving a low level of intervention. They were also educated to recognise when they needed to bring in a more highly trained specialist. In a similar way barefoot statisticians learn how to work within their local community or workplace. They work with groups to identify issues of common concern.

The barefoot statistician uses mathematical and statistical skills to collect, analyse and interpret all the relevant information. The community group then displays and communicates their conclusions to other concerned or affected people, or to those with responsibility and power in the situation. For example, a group of workers in an industry might gather data and argue a case for improving childcare facilities nearby; a student group might analyse student needs and put up a case for longer library hours; the residents of a suburb bordering an airport might produce evidence in favour of reducing airport noise; or a group of school students might put a case to the school's governing body, and to the local health authority, to have the community health nurse visit the school more often.

The barefoot statisticians know what statistical tools are available and when and how to use them, but they also know at what point they need to consult a more competent statistician, a software operator, or other specialist. They have the skills to act as first level consultants and to use mathematical techniques to describe, analyse and communicate, and in so doing help people define their own needs and solve their own problems.

Problem Posing as a Community Exercise

Social Constructivism also involves students taking a critical orientation towards mathematics. This includes an examination of both the explicit and implicit uses of mathematics, an identification of the value base upon which mathematics is built, and a study of the historical and social constraints on its development. Thus students take on the perspectives of the mathematics community, but do it with a measure of understanding about the place of mathematics in society.

The approach has shortcomings. It requires the teacher to be aware of the perspectives, approaches, attitudes and processes of the mathematical community, and the uses of mathematics in society (although this is not saying that the teacher has to be as technically proficient as a working mathematician).

Mathemacy and Reflective Knowing

Let me make a distinction between three types of knowing towards which a mathematics education can be oriented: (1) *Mathematical knowing*, which refers to the competence normally understood as mathematical skills including competences in reproducing theorems and proofs, as well as mastering a variety of algorithms. This competence is in focus in traditional mathematics education, and its importance has especially been stressed by the structuralistic or "new math" movement. (2) *Technological knowing*, which refers to abilities in applying mathematics, and to the competences of model building. The importance of technological knowing has been stressed by the applied oriented trend in mathematics education, maintaining that even if students learn mathematics, no guarantee exists that the developed competence is sufficient when it comes to situations of application. More has to be mastered than pure mathematics in order to apply mathematics. This extra competence, I shall call technological competence. More generally, it is the understanding necessary for using a technological tool in pursuing some technological aims. (3) *Reflective knowing*, which refers to the competence in reflecting upon and evaluating the use of mathematics. Reflections have to do with evaluations of the consequences of technological enterprises. . . . .

The fundamental thesis relating technological and reflective knowing is that technological knowing itself is unable to predict and analyse the results of its own production. Reflections are needed. Technological knowing is born shortsighted. Reflections must be based on a wider horizon of interpretations and pre-understandings. . . . . Technological and reflective knowing constitute two different types of knowledge, but not two independent types. It may be important to master some technological insight to support reflections. Even if we collect every bit of technological information, we shall not be able to build up reflections from those parts alone. While technological knowing aims at solving a problem, the object for reflections is an evaluation of a suggested technological solution of some (technological) problem.

Skovsmose (1994)

A Critical Approach to Mathematics

References

Agenda for Action. (1980). National Council of Teachers of Mathematics.

Beberman, M and Vaughan, H. (1964). *High School Mathematics.* Heath. Lexington, Massachusetts.

Bell, F. (1978). *Teaching and Learning Mathematics.* W. C. Brown Company Publishers.

Bishop, A. (1988). *Mathematical Enculturation* Kluwer Academic Publishers.

Cockcroft, W. (Ed). (1982). *Mathematics Counts.* HMSO.

Curriculum and Evaluation Standards for School Mathematics. (1989).

National Council of Teachers of Mathematics.

Ernest, P. (1991). *The Philosophy of Mathematics Education*. The Falmer Press.

Evans, J. (1986). *Statistics and Numeracy for Adults: the case for the 'barefoot statistician'*. Paper to ICOTS II, Victoria, Canada, August 1986.

Freudenthal, H. (1978). *Weeding and Sowing*. Dordrecht: Reidel.

Howson, A, Keitel, C and Kilpatrick, J. (1981). *Curriculum Development in Mathematics*. Cambridge: Cambridge University Press.

Howson, A. (1983). *Curriculum Development and Curriculum Research*. NFER-NELSON

Kamii, C. (1989). *Young Children Continue to Reivent Arithmetic*. Teachers College Press, Columbia University.

Neyland, J. (1995). Neo-behaviourism and Social Constructivism in Mathematics Education. *SAMEpapers 95*. Centre for Science and Mathematics Education Research, Waikato University.

Polya, G. (1945). *How to Solve it*. Princeton, NJ: Princeton University Press.

Resnick, L and Ford, W. (1984). *The Psychology of Mathematics for Instruction*. Lawrence Erlbaum. Hillsdale, New Jersey.

Resnick, L. (1989). Teaching Mathematics as an Ill-Structured Discipline. In Charles, R and Silver, E. (Eds). *The Teaching and Assessing of Mathematical Problem Solving*. NCTM.

Ritchie, G and Carr, K. (1992). A Constructivist Critique of Mastery Learning in Mathematics. *New Zealand Journal of Educational Studies*, 27(2), pp191-201.

Schoenfeld, A. (1992). Learning to Think Mathematically: Problem Solving, Metacognition, and Sense Making in Mathematics. In Grouws, D. (Ed). *Handbook of Research on Mathematics Teaching and Learning*. Macmillan: NY

Skovsmose, O. (1994). Towards a Critical Mathematics Education. *Educational Studies in Mathematics*. Vol 27, pp35-57.

5 The Challenge of Teaching for a Thinking Mathematics Classroom

Bronwen Cowie[1]

Focus Questions

- What is mathematics?
- What are the attributes of a mathematical thinker?
- How do I promote thinking in myself?
- How can I promote thinking in my classroom?

What is Mathematics?

This is not an easy question to answer. Everyone has experienced mathematics, at the very least at school, and has their own concept of it.

Reflection:
Pause now and reflect:

What is mathematics for me?
What are the essential qualities that make mathematics unique?

Here are some descriptions for you to consider:

[The] ability to calculate, to estimate and to reason logically. Mathematical problem solving involves the selection and correct application of basic skills, the discovery of patterns of shape and number, the making of models, the

---

[1] I am grateful to Jeanette Saunders for the time we have sent "thinking" about the issues discussed in this chapter.

interpretation of data and the recognition and communication of related ideas. The solution of mathematical problems requires creativity as well as a systematic approach. (*The New Zealand Curriculum Framework.*)

Mathematics provides powerful, precise and concise methods of representing patterns and relationships. It is characterised by activities such as defining, generalising, abstracting, analysing and proving. (The Australian Educational Council, 1991.)

Mathematics is effectively learned only by experimenting, questioning, reflecting, discovering, inventing and discussing. Thus for children, mathematics should be a kind of learning which requires a minimum of factual knowledge and a great deal of experience in dealing with situations using particular kinds of thinking skills. (Ahmed, 1987.)

Mathematics is a way of thinking... a systematic approach to quantitative and spatial problems. (Greenwood 1993.)

For this chapter I will treat mathematics as encompassing both a way of thinking and what is thought about. Looking for patterns, generalising and reasoning logically are important in many disciplines, but it is the nature of the patterns in mathematics that set it apart. Mathematical thinking uniquely arises from the analysis of number and spatial problems. This chapter offers a structure and suggestions for enhancing this thinking.

What are the attributes of a mathematical thinker?

Reflection:
Pause now think back to when you were last working on a mathematical question. Try to recapture what you thought, did and felt.

Now brainstorm endings to the sentence:

"A mathematical thinker . . . ."

Try for as many endings as you can, at least twenty. Adding verbs such as asks, does, speculates may help you get started.

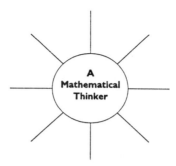

What is the same and what is different about a mathematical thinker and a thinker? (You may like to use a Venn diagram to aid your description.)

Here are some descriptions of mathematical thinking for you to compare and contrast with your own.

Mathematics in the New Zealand Curriculum (1992) affirms that problems which encourage thinking require a combination of skills, are non-routine, have multiple methods of solution and require flexibility and creativity.

Schoenfeld (1992) states:

Learning to think mathematically means (a) developing a mathematical point of view - valuing the processes of mathematization and abstraction and having the predilection to apply them, and (b) developing competence with the tools.

Mason, Burton and Stacey (1985) describe mathematical thinking as involving the processes of specialising, generalising, conjecturing and convincing.

A thinker is commonly characterised as someone who asks questions, takes risks, makes connections, is persistent, flexible and creative. A mathematical thinker has all these characteristics plus competence in and understanding of mathematical content and processes and the ability to identify where they are applicable.

Providing a Thinking Classroom

As mathematics teachers we usually focus on the mathematics in a lesson. If, as I believe, mathematics is more than a set of rules, formulae and procedures to be memorised we must also empower students to think mathematically. I use Fogarty and Bellanca's (1987) framework to help me deliberately foster thinking in my classes. This framework has four elements:

- teaching *with* thinking,
- teaching *of* thinking,
- teaching *about* thinking, and
- teaching *for* thinking.

Teaching *for* thinking means establishing a *climate* in which diversity is accepted and valued and risk taking is encouraged. Teaching *of* thinking involves specifically teaching and encouraging the use of thinking *skills* such as brainstorming, visualising, de Bono's "plus, minus and interesting" and "consider all factors". Teaching *with* thinking involves encouraging *interaction* through group work. Teaching *about* thinking involves helping students to think about their thinking, that is to use *metacognitive strategies*.

I have found these four elements are those which I use to promote my own thinking and I commend them as an excellent starting point when planning for mathematical thinking in your classroom.

If a thinking classroom is to be established, it is vital that we have a personal commitment to mathematics as a way of thinking, to being a thinker ourselves, and to promoting thinking in others. When these three aspects occur together we present mathematics as a subject which requires thought. We act as a role model of a mathematical thinker and facilitate mathematical thinking in our students.

Reflection:
Pause now and ask yourself:

What factors promote thinking in me? (You might like to use the diagram below to structure your response.)

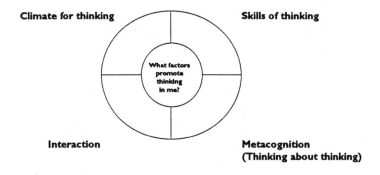

Questions for a Thinking Classroom

I have found one of the easiest ways of promoting thinking has been to alter and improve the questions I ask. It is through our questions and responses that we communicate to our students what mathematics is, what thinking it requires and what we value.

The classroom task is usually a question. It sets the scene for thinking and, ideally, will be accessible to all students, open, with multiple methods of solution and solutions which can then be shared and valued.

Opening Up Questions
A useful technique for opening up questions is to identify a topic, think of an answer and then make up a question which includes the answer (Ahmed, 1989, Sullivan and Clarke, 1991). Instead of "Find the perimeter of . . . ", we could ask "Draw some shapes with a perimeter of 24 cm".

Another technique is to *adapt* a question.

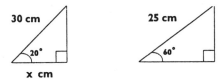

Instead of "Find x", we could ask "Find out all you can about this triangle".

Omitting some information from a typical question can open it up. "Mary has ¼ of a jar of jellybeans. How many jellybeans are there in the jar?"

Questions that Promote Thinking
"*What is the same and what is different?*" is my favourite question for promoting mathematical thinking. It encourages students to search for patterns and make connections between content and processes.

"What is the same and what is different about
*   34 x 12, 3.4 x 12, 3.4 x 1.2,
*   the graphs of y = 2x, y = 3x, y = -4x, y = 2x - 1, y = 2x + 5,
*   factorising and expanding,
*   the graph of y = x² - x - 6 and the solutions to x² - x - 6 = 0?"

A variation is to ask students to *"Compare and contrast"*

a rectangle, a square, a kite, a rhombus, a parallelogram, a triangle, a hexagon;

or to *"Group with reasons"*

$x^2 - 3x + 2$, $x^2 + 3x + 2$, $2x^2 + 3x + 1$, $x^2 - 9$, $x^2 + 3x$, $7x^2 + 3x - 2$.

"How do you know that....?" is another simple but powerful question that can be used to encourage students to think about and communicate their reasoning or to explore common misconceptions.

"How do you know that $x = 3$ is a solution to $2x + 1 = 7$?"
"How do you know that $3x^2$ is not equal to $(3x)^2$?"

"What if not.....?" can be used by both teachers and students to extend questions. First the attributes of a problem are listed, then the questioner asks "What if not..?" to change one of the attributes and hence produce a new question. Generating new questions like this requires students to think about the original question from a different perspective, to make new connections. Students can pose a variety of new questions, emphasising that there is no single "right" answer or question.

Find the rule for the pattern:

can be extended by asking
"What if the matches were arranged in squares?"
"What if they were in pentagons?"
"What if the triangles did not form a straight line?"

Any characteristic of the problem can be varied in order to produce a new question.

Students Posing Questions
As well as extending problems students learn by posing their own. To do so they need to analyse the essential elements of a question, process or skill, determine the contexts for which it is applicable and transfer this knowledge to a new situation. A simple idea is for students to

write the test and model answers for a topic. Material such as packaging, newspapers or the school grounds can act as a source of ideas for "real world" questions as can brainstorming mathematical questions we could ask about a random object such as a carrot, cone or balloon.

People Search
A "People Search" (Fogarty & Bellanca, 1987) is an excellent activity for encouraging a variety of responses. Students search for a different person to answer each question. An effective search relies on interaction, valuing prior knowledge, humour and the subtlety of language for its impact. It can be used to introduce or review a topic. A people search on probability could ask:

> Find someone who
> 1. is impossible,
> 2. can describe a tree,
> 3. can explain why although I've bought Lotto tickets I'm not a millionaire,
> 4. can estimate the probability of rain tomorrow.

The activity can be processed by asking students to report on the answers they received from others. The variety of experience and knowledge these answers produce can then be explored.

Starters For Higher Level Thinking Questions
Fogarty and Bellanca(1987) provide a list of "Three-Storey Verbs" which are useful when writing questions. These verbs can be used to raise the level of thinking required from the lower level of gathering ideas, to processing and interpreting them and then to transferring and using them. The following list of verbs is adapted from theirs.

Level 1 (Gathering): describe, name, count, recall, calculate.
Level 2 (Processing and interpreting): compare, contrast, explain why, analyse, distinguish.
Level 3 (Transferring and using): imagine, predict, speculate, if . . . then . . . . , estimate.

Questions on fraction division would change from "Calculate ½ ÷ ¼" to "Explain why we multiply by the reciprocal when we divide fractions", and finally "Predict which numbers we can use as divisors to produce a larger answer."

Helping without Telling

When students are working it is our role is to facilitate their thinking. The challenge in this is to help without telling because telling often involves doing the thinking for the student. One way to do this is to respond to a question with a question. I have found it useful to develop a standard set of response questions.

Questions which help students get started:
- What is the question asking?
- What do you already know about this?
- What could you try?

Questions for students who are stuck:
- What have you tried?
- What else could you try?
- Have you seen anything like this before?
- What is the question about?
- Can you draw a picture?

These questions focus on processes, not the answer, and indicate to students that these are what are valued. Students need time to make connections and see patterns so it is important they are given sufficient time to think through their response. My aim is for students to ask processing questions of themselves.

Reflection:

Pause now and consider:

If you communicate your view of mathematics to your students through the questions you ask, what do students' questions tell you about their view of mathematics?

Thinking Skills in a Thinking Classroom

By encouraging the use of thinking skills we can extend the range of processes students use when doing mathematics.

Brainstorming encourages students to recall all the associations they have already formed around an idea so that new links can be made. It is effective for generating possible strategies and exploring starting points when beginning work on a task.

Evaluating strategies, solutions and ways of thinking using "Plus, Minus and Interesting" develops students' ability to justify an answer, to analyze and accept diversity. This technique involves listing all the positive, negative and interesting points about an idea before making a judgement.

Reflection:
Pause now.

What would be the plus, minus and interesting factors in focusing on the thinking in a lesson?

Interactions in a Thinking Classroom

While working with others, students have opportunities to see and hear other ways of thinking, to build on the ideas of others and so to develop more elegant and effective solutions. Analytical questions such as "What is the same and what is different?", "How do you know that?" and "What if...?" arise naturally as they seek to make sense of the task and its solutions. Students need to clarify their thinking in order to explain it to others.

I use a combination of individual, paired and group work and particularly like the "Think, Pair, Share" strategy. In this students think by themselves for a few minutes and then pair up with someone else to share ideas. (Volume 1 of this book and Graves and Graves (1990) are useful resources for other cooperative learning techniques.)

Reflection:
Pause now.

What are the plus, minus and interesting aspects of working in a group for me? For students in my class?

Thinking about the Thinking

In a lesson which focuses on mathematical thinking it is important to help students think about both the mathematics and the thinking involved in an activity. The teacher acts as facilitator and a role model for this. Effective learning requires more than simply completing a task; the task needs to be processed to focus the learning.

The main time for processing tends to be after the activity when students can be encouraged to reflect on the mathematics they have experienced and the thinking they have used. Asking questions like
- How do you know you have answered the question? Are there more answers? Could you do it another way?
- What would you do the same and what would you do differently

next time?
* Where does this fit in? Is there anything you have learned
  today that you need to remember for next time?
* What if . . . . ?

encourages students to look for patterns and make connections back to
what they already know, to make sense of what they have been doing
and thinking. For more ideas on reflective thinking, see Chapter 36
of Volume 1 of this book.

Many of the "teaching points" of the lesson will arise as the
students report back on their answers to these questions and the
strategies and solutions they have found to the activity. This report-
back can become the main teaching time as we can build on student
feedback to ensure that the mathematics and the mathematical thinking
are fully appreciated and understood. Student thinking can be extended
by posing questions which require students to transfer or apply their
new knowledge.

In this environment errors are valuable as evidence of student
thinking. Asking students to look for patterns in and explain the errors
they make is an effective way to help them monitor their thinking.

Diagrams such as concept maps, Venn diagrams and matrices are
useful for illustrating the patterns and connections in what is being
learnt. Students can be asked to write down their responses to
reflecting questions. Both these techniques help students to make their
thinking visible.

We also have an important role in modelling mathematical
thinking. One way to do this is to think aloud while working through
problems.

Reflection:
Pause now and consider:

How would my lessons change if I did most of the teaching after
the students had worked on the activity?

Conclusion

An increased emphasis on mathematics as a way of thinking is
embedded in the *Mathematics in New Zealand Curriculum.* The
framework of teaching with, for, of and about thinking provides a
simple and effective way for implementing this emphasis in the
classroom.

By focusing on the thinking in my classroom I have been able to
shift my perspective. This has allowed me to generate and explore

different techniques for teaching and learning. I have encountered many challenges but my students and I have learned from and enjoyed the process.

How would you answer the question "Who is doing the thinking in this classroom?" I know my answer is "I am". I am working on ensuring my students can answer "We are".

Further Reading

Ahmed, A. (1987). *Better Mathematics: A Curriculum Development Study,* Her Majesty's Stationery Office, England.

de Bono, E. (1981) *CoRT - 1 Breadth.* Pergamon Press, Oxford.

Fogarty, R. and Bellanca, J. (1987). *Patterns for Thinking, Patterns for Transfer.* Hawker Brownlow Education, Australia.

Graves, N. and Graves, T. (1990). *A Part to Play.* Latitude Publications, Australia.

Greenwood, J. (1993). On the Nature of Teaching and Assessing "M athematical Power" and "Mathematical Thinking". *Arithmetic Teacher*, November pp144-152.

Mason, J. Burton, L. and Stacey, K. (1985). *Thinking Mathematically.* Addison-Wesley, England.

Schoenfeld, A.H. (1992). Learning to Think Mathematically: Problem Solving, Metacognition, and Sense Making in Mathematics. In D.A. Grouws (ed), *Handbook of Research on Mathematics Teaching and Learning.* MacMillan, New York.

Sullivan, P. (1992). *Open-ended Questions, Mathematical Investigations and the Role of the Teacher.* The Mathematical Association of Victoria, Melbourne.

Sullivan, P, Clarke, D, Spandel, U, and Wallbridge, M. (1992). *Using Content Specific Open Questions as a Basis of Instruction: A classroom Experiment.* ACU Christ Campus, Victoria.

Sullivan, P, Clarke, D. (1991). *Communication in the Classroom: The Importance of Good Questioning.* Deakin University, Victoria.

References

Australian Education Council. (1991). *A National Statement on Mathematics in Australian Schools.* Australian Education Council, Canberra.

Ministry of Education. (1992). *Mathematics in the New Zealand Curriculum.* Learning Media, Wellington.

Ministry of Education. (1993). *The New Zealand Curriculum Framework.* Learning Media, Wellington.

6   Constructivism in the Mathematics Classroom

Carol Mayers and Murray Britt

Introduction

The national curriculum statement *Mathematics in the New Zealand Curriculum* (1992, p12) states that, "as new experiences cause students to refine their existing knowledge and ideas, so they construct new knowledge." The theory that argues for this view of learning is known as constructivism. Constructivists believe that "learners actively construct their own understandings rather than passively absorb or copy the understandings of others" (Simon and Schifter, 1991, p310). Thus the teachers' concepts cannot be transferred directly to the learner. Instead, the teacher strives "to maximise opportunities for students to construct concepts" and to "give fewer explanations and expect less memorisation and imitation" (Simon and Schifter, 1991, p325). So, what does this mean for the mathematics teacher? This chapter outlines some of the implications of this theory for the classroom. But firstly, let us look at an example that illustrates some of the differences between constructivist and non-constructivist approaches.

Into the Classroom

A group of teachers was asked to present the following task to their students (see Mousley, 1992).

From a given piece of cardboard, make a regular shape which holds one cup of birdseed. When you have done this, make a similar shape that is twice as big.

Teacher A presented the task in its original form while others (teachers B and C) who believed that the task was too vague and that their

J. Neyland (ed), Mathematics Education: A Handbook for Teachers, Vol.2, 60-69
© *1995 Wellington College of Education: New Zealand*

students might not discover the important mathematical ideas, modified it as follows.

Teacher B: Make a box which holds one cup of birdseed and then make another box which is twice as big.

Teacher C: Make a cube 5 cm by 5 cm by 5 cm. Make another cube 10 cm by 10 cm by 10 cm. Compare the volumes of the two cubes.

By making this adjustment, teacher B planned to increase her students' understanding of the formula for the volume of a cube. Teacher C wanted her students to discover that if the dimensions of a cube are doubled, the volume will increase to 8 times the original volume. It is evident that these teachers wanted their students to take a relatively direct path of 'discovery'. This teacher expectation led to a corresponding student one. The students in both classes appeared to expect the teacher to lead them towards her solution, and acted accordingly. They engaged in the task with little enthusiasm and continually asked the teacher for explanations and for confirmation that they were doing the task correctly. Whilst the teachers thought the modified tasks mathematically interesting, their students showed little 'ownership'. They thought that it mattered little whether or not they 'discovered' the intended mathematical ideas, because they knew that at the end of the lesson the teacher would explain them anyway (see Britt et al., 1993 pp70-75).

Burkhardt and Fraser (1992) suggest that, for 'guided discovery' approaches, the students believe the mathematics is 'in the teacher's head' and that 'guided discovery' is therefore little more than teacher explanation. For such an approach, the teacher's task is to devise a learning path which leads directly to the planned lesson outcomes.

Teacher A, by contrast, saw opportunities for the students to take ownership of their own mathematical activity, and left it much more open for individual student interpretations. Her students produced a range of shapes: cylinders, cones, pyramids, cubes and cuboids, and discovered a wide variety of mathematical ideas, which included the ideas that teachers B and C had wanted to develop. The students in this class appeared to believe in their ability to solve problems for themselves. They participated in prolonged small group and whole-class discussions and co-operated to clarify and solve the task. They saw the process of problem solving as 'discovering meaning', as opposed to 'finding out about the teacher's mathematical ideas'.

By leaving the task open, teacher A provided her students with opportunities to engage in mathematical exploration that might result in mental conflict, or 'disequilibrium', between new and existing ideas. The resolution of this conflict requires a process of sustained mental activity through which mental connections are made between concepts. Disequilibrium can only be resolved by mental activity. The learners modify their cognitive schemata to accommodate new ideas. Teacher A had a crucial role in helping her students resolve these 'conflicts' between new and existing ideas. She listened to their suggestions and explanations and directed the discussion and reflection towards the conflicting ideas using 'open' questions and paraphrases of their explanations. For teachers B and C, the students were required to follow the path set by the teacher. Whilst there were opportunities for these students to refine (and even reject) existing ideas as they progressed along the path, such opportunities occurred largely by chance, and for many, not at all.

The Role of the Teacher

Let us examine the teacher's role in more detail. Von Glasersfeld (quoted in Cobb and Wood, 1990, p34), highlights the need for a change in teachers' perceptions of their role when he says "teaching becomes a very different proposition from the traditional notion where knowledge is in the head of the teacher and the teacher has to find ways of conveying it or transferring it to the student." Within a constructivist pedagogy, the teacher is a facilitator of learning. She provides situations in which the students can engage in collaborative mathematical problem-solving in small groups where they have opportunities to discuss, explain and justify their solutions. She facilitates whole-class discussions of problems, interpretations and solutions. She has the responsibility to create a 'problem-solving atmosphere' (Cobb et al., 1988; Yackel and Wheatley, 1990); to facilitate mathematical 'talk' (Cobb and Wood, 1990); to create a social climate conducive to effective problem-solving and productive mathematical 'talk' (Yackel and Wheatley, 1990; Cobb et al., 1988; Cobb et al., 1991); to design appropriate tasks to stimulate mental activity (Cobb and Wood, 1990; Mousley, 1992); to develop their own curricula (Steffe, 1990a; Maher, Davis and Alston, 1992); and to develop new approaches to assessment (Maher and Alston, 1990; Carr and Ritchie, 1991).

Creating a Problem Solving Atmosphere. What is a problem solving atmosphere? It is one in which students persist in their attempts to solve problems which they view as personal challenges; in which students believe mathematics should make sense; in which students are active participants in creating their own mathematics; in which students feel free to discuss their ideas in small groups and whole-class discussion; and in which students "accept that their solutions should be explainable and justifiable" (Cobb et al., 1988, p46). Students are expected, not only to verbalise their own ideas, but to reflect upon and respond to those of other students (Yackel and Wheatley, 1990).

Discussion:
Reflect on the factors which help create a problem solving atmosphere.
- Which of these factors can you recall making a significant contribution to effective learning in mathematics?
- How can you incorporate each of these factors into your classroom environment?

Facilitating Mathematical 'Talk'. The teacher has an important role in facilitating mathematical 'talk', through small-group and whole-class discussions, in which the focus is on 'developing meaning' as opposed to 'getting correct answers' (Yackel and Wheatley, 1990). Typically in constructivist classrooms, students are given problems to solve collaboratively, in pairs or small groups. They work together to resolve differences in their interpretations of the problems and in their approaches to solving them. Individual students attempt to develop explanations that are meaningful to others and attempt to interpret and make sense of other people's ideas. These attempts to verbalise and interpret partially formed ideas constitute 'exploratory' talk as opposed to 'final draft' talk (Cobb and Wood, 1990).

During subsequent whole-class discussion, students are expected to give more coherent explanations of the outcomes of their small group's efforts and to respond to questions and challenges from their peers. They are also expected to listen to, and try to make sense of, other people's explanations, and to ask appropriate questions and seek clarification. It is argued that when children engage in this type of mathematical 'talk', it can result in "learning opportunities that rarely arise in traditional instructional settings" (Cobb and Wood, 1990, p35). Students learn to reason analytically and to communicate by explaining and justifying their mathematical ideas.

The teacher's role is to facilitate this type of mathematical 'talk' by helping students to express their mathematical thinking and by encouraging them to conceptualise situations in different ways. She asks probing questions, requests paraphrases of ideas, focuses the discussion as needed (Simon and Schifter, 1991), and highlights significant aspects of the students' mathematical contributions (Cobb and Wood, 1990). She encourages the students to explore misconceptions and conflicting ideas in order that they will develop 'broader more resilient concepts' (Simon and Schifter, 1991, p311). She paraphrases the students' explanations so that their emerging mathematical ideas will become more robust. In these ways the teacher guides the development of 'taken-to-be-shared' mathematical understandings (Cobb and Wood, 1990), and the development of 'bridges' between the mathematics of the classroom and the abstract concepts and procedures of the formalised mathematics of the community (Simon and Schifter, 1991). "The teacher's role in initiating and guiding mathematical negotiations is a highly complex one." (Cobb et al., 1991, p7)

Discussion:
To facilitate the kind of mathematical 'talk' described above, teachers need to develop expertise in listening to students as they engage in such 'talk' and in observing students' actions as they attempt to resolve problem situations. And they need to know the mathematics that might emerge during students' activity (Steffe, 1990b).
- How can you develop your listening and observational skills?
- How can you increase your mathematical knowledge, thus enabling you to make better sense of students' 'talk'?

Creating an Appropriate Social Climate. The teacher has a responsibility to establish a social climate within the classroom which is conducive to effective problem solving and to productive mathematical 'talk'. This requires, among other things, that the teacher clearly articulates her expectation that the students will assume some responsibility for their own learning and conduct (Cobb et al., 1988). For example, the teacher may encourage the students to take a pride in their own achievements, and specify that they have the responsibility to think through and make sense of tasks presented to them and to explain their ideas and solution attempts.

In addition to making clear statements of expectations, teachers have to accept certain obligations for themselves if they are to successfully create problem solving environments. It is important for teachers to demonstrate to their students that they have a genuine interest in their mathematical thinking; that they value their efforts, and that both students and teacher can learn from errors arising from attempts to solve problems. It is therefore important that teachers accept students' explanations and justifications in a non-evaluative way, so that they feel "comfortable to respond freely and to express their ideas" (Yackel and Wheatley, 1990, p58). Thus, classroom environments which are conducive to problem solving and to productive mathematical 'talk' are characterised by a "trust between the teacher and pupils" (Yackel and Wheatley, 1990, p58).

It is important that the teacher establish classroom social norms which enable the students to engage in productive group work without needing constant teacher monitoring (Cobb et al., 1991), and which enable students to participate productively in whole-class discussion. Social norms for small group work include: persist when solving challenging problems; explain personal solutions within the group setting; listen to and try to make sense of explanations made by other group members; attempt to reach consensus about an answer, and ideally a solution process, in situations where a conflict between interpretations or solutions has become apparent (Cobb et al., 1991). Social norms for whole-class discussion include: explain and justify your solutions; try to make sense of the explanations given by others; indicate agreement or disagreement; and question alternatives in situations where a conflict between interpretations or solutions has become apparent (Cobb et al., 1991).

Discussion:
Creating a social climate in the ways described above is an aspect of teaching that is often referred to as classroom organisation and management. The skills required for ongoing success in this area of teaching develop over time.
- Reflect on your experiences in this area and make a list of ideas you can try out in the near future.
- Make a list of ways you can monitor your own progress in the area of classroom organisation and management.

Designing Learning Situations. The teacher has the critical task of selecting and developing learning activities which are accessible to groups of students with a range of conceptual levels, and which help each of them learn. Cobb and Wood (1990) highlight important differences between the constructivist approach and that of 'guided discovery'. The guided discovery approach usually starts with a mathematical analysis of the relationships the teacher wants the students to discover. It then presents these relationships to the students via a series of embodiments, often using manipulative materials or activities. The constructivist approach on the other hand, acknowledges that individual students interpret problem situations uniquely. Thus instead of a mathematical analysis, it is the teacher's understanding of the students' mathematical ideas which is the starting point. Learning activities are not designed so that every student makes the same mathematical constructions or understands the same relationships. Rather, they are designed with the aim of helping students with a range of prior understandings learn new mathematical ideas. Because it is recognised that learning occurs when students attempt to resolve cognitive conflicts, activities are included which have the potential to create these problematic situations (Cobb and Wood, 1990).

This notion is illustrated well by the task considered at the beginning of this chapter. Whilst the open nature of the task allows for a range of mathematical ideas to emerge, it also allows for a wide range of entry points for students working at different conceptual levels. For example, some students may use trial and error methods to reach a satisfactory solution, and others with different prior knowledge may draw out more sophisticated ideas such as scale factor for enlargement. In such a problem, the 'apparent' vagueness of the task is in fact a strength.

Discussion:
It is not easy to design classroom activities that both engage and challenge a range of students. Whilst few texts include tasks of the kind described above, it is possible to modify textbook problems to make them more 'open'.
- Look through textbooks for problem situations that have this potential.
- Use these to design mathematical tasks that are both open and challenging in the manner described above.
- List the mathematical ideas that you think might be drawn from the task.

Developing Classroom Curricula. Constructivist approaches require the teacher to tailor the learning environment to the learning needs of the students. Accordingly, the teacher needs to take an active role in curriculum development at the classroom level and cannot be driven by externally prescribed curriculum documents, such as school schemes or national syllabi (Steffe, 1990). Just as constructivism requires students to take responsibility for their own learning, it requires teachers to take responsibility for their own teaching. Thus Steffe (1990a) rejects the traditional 'top-down' curriculum, and instead asserts that teachers need to work within general curriculum guidelines and shape in the details, in response to their students, as they work. He argues that a curriculum should not be seen as a fixed entity, independent of individual students and teachers, but as starting points that must undergo transformation during actual teaching. Thus, teachers should create (or at least modify) the curriculum as they interact with the students and come to make sense of their current conceptions. Maher, Davis and Alston (1992) also highlight the need for a flexible curriculum. They claim that it is only when teachers have flexibility within their overall plan that they are able to respond to students' idiosyncratic interpretations, cognitive conflicts and emerging understandings.

Devising Appropriate Methods of Assessment. If mathematics is to be presented as a 'way of knowing' rather than as an end-product, assessment methods must change too. Carr and Ritchie (1991) highlight some of the limitations of existing methods of assessment. They found that written tests, which usually test only a narrow range of skills and procedures, do not provide a realistic indication of what the students know, and that follow-up interviews are needed to give a reasonable picture of mathematical understanding. Moreover, written tests do not take account of the strategy shifts students may show. Two students may get the same answer but use different strategies, and thus indicate marked differences in knowledge and understanding. Several studies (e.g., Carpenter et al., 1989) have shown that young children can solve real-world problems which the results of paper and pencil tests would predict they cannot. Thus, whilst written tests may show that children can solve 'school maths' problems, they do not indicate a child's ability to solve problems in a wider context. There is, suggest Carr and Ritchie (1991), a further danger that "assessment can hijack the curriculum". If teachers believe that test-based assessment provides a good indication of the learner's knowledge and understanding, then the curriculum can become oriented to the test; teachers will "teach to the test".

Carr and Ritchie (1991) propose that constructivist approaches to assessment should emphasise the involvement of the students in assessing their own learning, and that the teacher's role is to assist the students in their efforts to assess what they have learnt. For example, students may be asked to describe to the teacher or to their peers how they solved problems. In this way the teacher gains ideas about the mathematical ideas and strategies of the learner, and the students learn about what they know and understand, and when their knowledge and understanding is insufficient to solve a problem. Thus assessment becomes an integral part of the teaching-learning process. Carr and Ritchie (1991, p3) conclude by suggesting that "only by observing and listening to learners as they solve mathematical problems and pursue investigations can we get the type of information that will help us plan for better learning."

Conclusion

The role of the teacher who is committed to constructivist approaches is not only different from that of the traditional teacher, but considerably more demanding. Teachers need to know the mathematics they are teaching and be confident enough to release the control of the learning to the students. To a very real extent they are co-learners with their students. They therefore need to see themselves as taking on roles of being both expert and novice at different moments. The teacher's craft is to recognise when their expertise is required and how that expertise can be used to maximise learning.

References

Britt, M. S., Irwin, K. C., Ellis, J. and Ritchie, G. (1993). *Report on the teachers raising achievement in mathematics project.* Auckland: Centre for Mathematics Education, Auckland College of Education.

Burkhardt, H. and Fraser, R. (1992). An overview. In B. Cornu and A. Ralston (Eds.) *Science and technology education 44. The influence of computers and informatics on mathematics and its teaching.* Paris: UNESCO.

Carpenter, T. P., Fennema, E., Peterson, P. L., Chiang, C., and Loef, M. (1989) *Using knowledge of students' mathematical thinking in classroom teaching: An experimental study.* American Educational Research Journal. 26, 499-532.

Carr, K. and Ritchie, G. (1991). Evaluating learning in mathematics. *SET*, 1 Item 15, 1-4.

Cobb, P., Yackel, E., Wood, T., and Wheatley, G. (1988). Creating a problem solving atmosphere. *Arithmetic Teacher.* 36, (1), 46-47.

Cobb, P., and Wood, T. (1990). Experience, problem solving, and discourse as central aspects of constructivism. *Arithmetic Teacher.* 38, (4), 34-35.

Cobb, P., Wood, T., Yackel, E., Nicholls, J., Wheatley, G., Trigatti, B., and Perlwitz, M., (1991) Assessment of a problem-centered second-grade mathematics project. Journal for Research in Mathematics Education. 22, (1), 3-29.

Maher, C. A., Alston, A. (1990). Teacher development in mathematics in a constructivist framework. In Davis, R. B., Maher, C. A., Noddings, N. (Eds.) *Constructivist views on the teaching and learning of mathematics. Reston,* VA: National Council of Teachers of Mathematics.

Maher, C. A., Davis, R. B., and Alston, A. (1992). Teachers paying attention to students' thinking. *Arithmetic Teacher*, 39, (9), 34-37.

Mousley, J. A. (1992). *Constructivism: epistemology to practice*. Paper presented at MERGA conference, Sydney, Australia.

Ministry of Education. (1992). *Mathematics in the New Zealand Curriculum*. Wellington: Ministry of Education.

Simon, M. and Schifter, D. (1991). Towards a constructivist perspective: An intervention study of mathematics teacher development. *Educational Studies in Mathematics*, 22, (4) 309-331.

Steffe, L. P. (1990a). Mathematics curriculum design: A constructivist's perspective. In Steffe, L. P., Wood, T. (Eds.) *Transforming students' mathematical education: International perspectives*. Hillsdale, NJ: Lawrence Erlbaum Associates.

Steffe, L. P. (1990b). On the knowledge of mathematics teachers. In Davis, R. B., Maher, C. A., Noddings, N. (Eds) *Constructivist views on the teaching and learning of mathematics*. Reston, VA: National Council of Teachers of Mathematics.

Yackel, E. and Wheatley, G. R. (1990). Promoting visual imagery in young students. *Arithmetic Teacher*, 37, (6), 52-58.

7   Making Sense when Learning Mathematics

Andy Begg

Discussion Questions

- Reflecting on your own experiences: How did you learn at school? How do you learn now? How did your most effective teachers help you learn?
- Recall times when: (i) You rejected old ideas because they did not fit with your new ideas; (ii) You rejected new ideas because you did not feel comfortable with them; (iii) You battled to reconcile your pre-conceived ideas with new information.
- Can you think of an example where you know something to be true, but you conveniently use some other idea as good enough even when it is not true?
- What are the practical difficulties associated with: (i) Accommodating students' prior ideas; (ii) Allowing students to investigate their own questions; (iii) Assessment, when students are investigating topics in their own way?

Introduction

Most mathematics teachers in schools, and mathematics education lecturers in colleges of education and universities, met some of the following buzz words when they learnt about education: drill and practice, behavioural objectives, discovery learning, Piaget's ages and stages, investigations and projects, individualised programmes, and mastery learning. These words were based on the theories and research findings about learning that were current at the time. The new buzz word is constructivism. Constructivism is a way of describing how people come to know what they know; that is, how they learn, and how they make sense of their world. This buzz word is more than a fad. It is based on research and its key concepts are useful for explaining how our students learn, and for analysing our approaches to teaching.

Constructivism

Constructivism is a theory of knowing and learning, rather than a theory of teaching. Ernst von Glasersfeld (1989) is one of its principal proponents and he traces its formulation to Giambattista Vico in 1710. Von Glasersfeld (1989) asserts that constructivism is based on two key principles. Paraphrased these are:

(i) knowledge is not passively received, but actively built up, by a thinking learner; and

(ii) thinking is an adaptive process that helps the learner to organize his or her experiential world, rather than to know absolute reality.

Passive reception or active construction?

The first of these principles states something which most teachers know from experience - students do not learn by merely attending class. Learners need to actively think about and process the ideas they meet. This thinking and processing is more likely to occur if they are involved in experimenting, forming and investigating hypotheses, and validating their ideas through learning activities, than if they are just sitting and listening. This is not a new idea. It is similar to the well established Socratic method and to the educational approaches promoted by the philosopher-educator John Dewey. The learning activity referred to includes, not only critical thinking, but social interaction between teacher and learners, and between learners. Through these social transactions learners develop their ideas by modifying them in the light of the conflicting views of others, and by justifying and explaining their thinking to others. Theories of learning and knowing which acknowledge the importance of social transaction and negotiation are sometimes referred to as social constructivist theories. Thus, for these constructivist and social constructivist theories, language is an important tool for aiding the student's construction of knowledge through social interaction, but it cannot substitute for the student's own thinking activity. And knowledge cannot simply be transferred from the teacher to the student by linguistic communication.

Adaptive Process

The second key principle refers to an adaptive process. This occurs when students take on new ideas and link them with their prior beliefs, experiences and understandings. The prior ideas influence learning by providing the lens through which new ideas are viewed. Adaption may occur in a number of ways. If the new ideas do not conflict with the prior ideas, then they may be integrated with them. If the new ideas conflict with prior knowledge, then they may be accepted, with the earlier ideas taking either an inferior or a superior status. If the status of the new ideas is too low then they may be rejected.

The form of adaption used is likely to depend on whether the learner is dissatisfied with his or her existing ideas, and whether the new ideas seem intelligible, plausible and fruitful (Posner, Strike, Hewson and Gertzog, 1982).

When integration does not occur, the learner may compartmentalize the conflicting ideas. For example, if a learner has a system for multiplying numbers using repeated addition, and the teacher is introducing long multiplication, one system may be seen by the student as real knowledge while the other may be compartmentalized as unreal or 'school' knowledge. Thus, one is given inferior status. Because the student's prior ideas (alternative ideas, naive views, errors or misconceptions) are so influential in the adaptation process, it is important for the teacher to be aware of them and work to make any conflicts between them and newer ideas explicit. Thus, teachers need to focus on what seems to be going on inside students' heads, rather than on their overt 'responses' as this is likely to give them a better insight into how the new ideas are being adapted. In particular, teachers need to be interested in students' 'errors' and in any deviations from the intended path, because these throw light on how they, at this point in their development, are organizing their ideas.

Organising experience or knowing reality?

Does knowing mean having an absolute understanding, or is it having a view that 'fits' with experiences and 'makes sense' of them? I would suggest that it is the latter of these two. Imagine a work of art and the different views the artist, geometer, historian, art dealer, and investor have. Are all these perspectives essential for knowledge? Can any one person say they have the right view? This is an example of people organising their experiences in different ways. They each know about the work of art, but their knowledge in not absolute. Each person's knowledge is a construction which 'fits' with their experiences.

Mathematics, too, is a human construction, an invention of people. It does not exist in its own right but provides ways of organising and making sense of the world. Languages are also human constructions. Often words in one language have shades of meaning with no equivalent in other languages, and thus one's knowledge is dependent on one's prior language experiences.

This view of knowledge as being a 'good fit', to make sense of one's world, rather than 'absolute truth', does not mean that there is not sometimes a right and a wrong view. It means that right and wrong are relative terms. When we say that students have the right idea we mean they have the socially accepted view that the teachers had intended. Some critics of constructivism, often people with a belief in the infallibility of truth and the knower's ability to know absolute reality, suggest that constructivists believe that no absolute reality exists, and that for the constructivist all constructions are equally valid. This is a misconception that was not intended by constructivists. Constructivists do not claim that no reality exists, they only claim that one cannot directly know this reality.

Teaching

We observed earlier that constructivism is about learning, not teaching. However, a number of educators have contributed to the development of teaching models in line with constructivist principles. These include Osborne and Wittrock's (1983) *Generative* model, Biddulph and Osborne's (1984) *Interactive* model, and Wheatley's (1991) *Problem-solving* model. Now it must be acknowledged that if one accepts constructivism as a theory of learning then one assumes that students construct their knowledge according to these principles whenever they learn, regardless of how they are taught. However, a skilled teacher can make the process more effective, and these models are designed to help teachers develop these skills.

Interactive Teaching Model

The Interactive teaching model was developed in New Zealand by Biddulph and Osborne (1984). It is used by many primary teachers, some science teachers, and a smaller number of mathematics teachers. In interactive teaching the teacher endeavours when teaching a topic:
- to take into account each student's prior thinking about the topic;
- to become more sensitive to the children's ideas and questions and to provide exploratory experiences from which they can raise

useful questions and suggest sensible explanations;
- to introduce activities that focus on the questions and ideas that many of the children had;
- to act as a team research leader with the students to help them plan and carry out investigations into their questions and to help them draw sensible and useful conclusions from their findings. This requires the teacher to develop the skill of interacting with the children to challenge, modify and extend their ideas, instead of leaving it to the children to make of their experiences what they will, or dogmatically imposing on them answers to their questions.

The Interactive teaching model implies a role shift for teachers which makes more demands on them than traditional chalk-and-talk approaches. It involves a shift from a focus on well-defined objectives which can easily be assessed, to the provision of rich learning activities centred on the students' interests. The expectation is that students grow from where they are, that they construct or modify their own ideas, that they will be empowered to seek their own solutions rather than follow a path totally determined by the teacher, and that the learning outcome may be different for each student. The interactive teaching approach also suggests the students should have a role in negotiating their curriculum.

Assessment

Teachers who view learning from a constructivist perspective need to consider what assessment feedback they and their students need (Begg, 1991). Assessment arises in three situations and answers questions such as:
(i) before teaching a topic
- what are the children's interests in this topic?
- what are their current ideas, their conceptions and misconceptions?
- what questions are they likely to have about this topic?
- what learning activities are suitable for focusing on these questions?
(ii) during learning
- what are the children's actual questions?
- are the learning activities focusing on these questions?
- are the meanings that the children are constructing similar to the intended ones?
- how are the children putting together their ideas, what are they thinking?

(iii) after the topic is covered
- what are the children's ideas when the topic is completed?
- are these ideas different from their earlier views?
- what needs to be reported or recorded for student documentation?

Assessment may be done informally by questioning and observing while the students are planning their explorations and investigating their questions. The teacher's role would be one of challenger, supporter, and encourager, using 'what if' and 'what if not' questions, and other questions that respected the learners and their views but helped them construct alternative ideas and consider different conclusions. Teachers might use other assessment techniques too, such as, interviews, surveys, concept maps, and postbox techniques - these are described in detail by Bell (1993).

The 'after learning' or summative assessment will be difficult. The obvious problem is, how do we measure conceptual change? That is, how do we compare earlier with later conceptions? This will be more difficult when the curriculum has been freely negotiated and when the activities and problems vary for each group of learners.

Curriculum

Those who believe that a national curriculum, or school scheme, should outline specific achievement objectives for all students of each particular age, find behaviourist learning theories appealing. By contrast, a constructivist curriculum or scheme needs to be more open-ended, respect the autonomy of the students, and rely on the professionalism of teachers. Unfortunately new curriculums are often designed using student-centred and constructivist views about learning, but, because of national assessment policies, have assessment tasks linked to them that fit with the contrasting behaviourist views.

Conclusion

Constructivism is useful because it explains what happens in classrooms better than older theories. It is gaining international acceptance among mathematics educators. Constructivism raises important questions about learning, teaching, assessment and course design, and offers no simple solutions to these questions. The challenge for teachers is to find an approach to teaching, learning, assessment, and course design that makes sense of their own professional experiences, observations and reflections. This is an ongoing process.

References

Begg, A J C (1991). *Assessment and Constructivism.* Paper presented at the ICMI Study Conference on Assessment in Mathematics Education and its Effects, Spain, April 1991.

Bell, B F (1993). *Taking Into Account Students' Thinking: A teacher development guide,* Hamilton: Centre for Science and Mathematics Education Research, University of Waikato.

Biddulph, F and Osborne, R J (eds) (1984). *Making Sense of Our World: an interactive teaching approach.* Hamilton: Centre for Science and Mathematics Education Research, University of Waikato.

Osborne, R J and Wittrock, M C (1983). Learning science: a generative process, *Science Education* 67(4), 489-508.

Posner, G J, Strike, K A, Hewson, P E and Gertzog, W A (1982). Accommodation of a Scientific Conception: Towards a Theory of Conceptual Change, *Science Education* 66(2), 211-227.

Vico, G (1710). *De antiquissima Italorum sapientia.* Naples: Felice Mosca. (Cited in von Glasersfeld, 1989).

von Glasersfeld, E (1989). Constructivism in Education. In the *International Encyclopaedia of Education: Research and Studies,* Supplementary Volume. Oxford: Pergamon Press.

Wheatley, G H (1991). Constructivist Perspectives on Science and Mathematics Learning, *Science Education* 75(1), 9-21.

Planning, Assessment and Evaluation

8   The Teacher's Influence

Elaine Mayo

Introduction

As a teacher, are you free to teach what you like, how you like? Clearly not. Are you tightly controlled and told exactly what to teach each period, and how to teach it? Clearly not. Are you expected to be accountable for your teaching? Yes, you are; you are accountable to your managers and your students, and they are accountable to you.

This chapter sets out to clarify the nature of the responsibilities and accountabilities in the New Zealand Education system. The first section discusses (i) the factors which influence the way a teacher plans, and (ii) the ways in which teachers can influence the education system.

The second section shows how the principles of teacher planning apply equally to other groups in the education system. This leads to a description of the chain of accountability which is central to our New Zealand Education system.

Finally I shall make some comparisons between the current system and the way education was administered before the restructuring of the education system in 1989. I suggest that some schools and teachers might be experiencing problems because they have not yet become skilled at planning within the new system.

Influences in Teaching

What follows is an activity in which you are asked to sort out some of the things that affect what and how you teach.

Activity.
Jot down a list of the main things that influence your planning and your actions as a teacher. Some influences are so accepted they are not even noticed. To spot some of these subtle influences think about *when, where, who, what, how,* and *why* you teach. Sort your list into the following three categories.

J. Neyland (ed), Mathematics Education: A Handbook for Teachers, Vol.2, 78-85
© 1995 Wellington College of Education: New Zealand

(1) Those influences that are a result of where you teach. This category will include all the New Zealand legal requirements and curriculum statements, your school wide policies and procedures, and the content of your school or department scheme.

A Planning Cycle with Inputs and Outputs

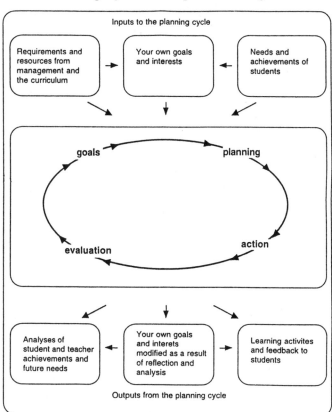

Diagram 1

(2) Those influences that are a result of who you teach. This category will include all the things you know about your students, the results of your assessment of their understanding, their needs, their behaviour, and their desire to learn.

(3) Those influences that are a result of your own understanding of education and how people learn, your own confidence and skill as a teacher, your beliefs and values about what is important in education, and your understanding of your curriculum area. Include

in this category any item you did not include in either the first or second category.

Diagram 1 incorporates these three classes of factors as inputs into a planning loop which cycles around four stages: identifying goals, planning actions, carrying out the plan, and evaluating the effectiveness the whole process in preparation for the next circuit around the loop. A thorough understanding of the nature of each of these input factors will increase the chance that you will be able to operate effectively and independently in our education system.

In this situation, 'influence' works both ways. Not only do external requirements, teacher beliefs and student needs affect the actions of the teacher, but the teacher can, in return, modify the nature of these factors. The reverse component of the influence relation is shown at the bottom of Diagram 1 as outputs from the planning loop. I believe that many teachers do not understand, and make use of, their power to inform and influence their managers, students, parents, and local community.

The next activity is similar to the first one. This time you are being asked to note (i) the ways in which you inform others about your work and what you need and expect from them in order to do your job well, and (ii) the ways you challenge your own beliefs and understandings.

Activity.
Jot down a list of the main ways that you influence yourself and others as a result of your planning, actions, evaluations and personal development as a teacher. Sort your list into three categories.

(1) Those influences that affect the institution in which you teach. This category will include (i) any work you do that contributes to school wide policies and procedures, or the contents of your school or department scheme, (ii) the analyses you do of student achievement, and the requests and recommendations you make to management for additional resources and for teacher development opportunities, and (iii) your contributions to reports to management and the Board of Trustees about the effectiveness of programmes in the school.

(2) Those influences that affect the students you teach. This category will include all the things you plan for in order to help learning: all the teaching and assessment activities, the ways in which you coach students to help them learn, the feedback you give them about their progress, the marking you do, and the reports you write.

(3) The ways you alter your own understanding of teaching and learning, and the ways you as a citizen affect those around you (your friends, your colleagues, your community, and your politicians). This category will include all the contributions you make to education by being active in subject associations, teacher unions, and your community. It will include all the ways in which you evaluate and adjust your own beliefs and develop your skills.

A thorough understanding of how the outputs from the planning cycle can contribute to an empowered teaching community will help you understand how to effect change within education. How do you make changes to your own thinking as a result of reading, discussion and reflection? How do you influence the thinking of others through the teaching and learning process, and through the process of evaluating teaching and providing feedback to management? An understanding of the answers to these questions can lead to action for change.

Influences in Education

Other groups in the education system have similar planning and influence cycles. Diagram 2 shows some of these. The left-hand column shows the requirements and funding constraints which affect teachers and schools. The state through the Ministry of Education, for example, requires Boards of Trustees to comply with the 'National Administration Guidelines' and it provides funding to the Board of Trustees to run the school. The board is required to prepare a budget and to ensure that certain requirements are met. This is commonly done by setting policy in place and delegating the implementation of the policy to the managers in the school. Managers in schools pass on the responsibility and funding to teachers, and teachers translate these into teaching activities and resources.

The right-hand column shows the ways in which information flows back through the chain from student to teacher, teacher to manager, manager to board, and board to state. The information flowing this way is information about achievements and needs. A good flow of information is essential for effective planning. If for example, a teacher is not aware of the needs of her students then her planning will be inadequate. If a Board of Trustees does not know about the teachers' professional development needs, or their work loads, then it will not be able to plan adequately, and it will be unable to properly report on the stresses and pressures within the education system.

Responsibilities	Accountabilities
The State and the Community	
Schools are given funding and required to operate in accordance with the law. Requirements include the Charter, the National Educational Guidelines, the National Administrative Guidelines and the National Curriculum.	The Annual report of the Board of Trustees to the community contains financial statements and reports about school operations and achievements. A copy goes to the Minister of Education. How can the Board give better feedback to the State and the Community?
The Board of Trustees	
The Board of Trustees writes policy. It establishes annual priorities and lays out a budget for key operations. It is responsible for such things as staffing, property maintenance and for monitoring the effectiveness of curriculum delivery.	Managers collect and analyze their own achievements and needs, and those of teachers and students and report these to the Board of Trustees. How can management give better feedback to Trustees?
School Management The Principal and Heads of Departments	
School managers operate within the policies set by the Board. They establish the operating procedures that will be used in the school (the timetable, schemes of work, the ways staff will be involved in planning and budgeting in their departments).	Teachers analyze the achievements and needs of their students and give feedback to their managers about that and their own professional needs and achievements. How can teachers give better feedback to management?
Teachers	
Teachers work to management's procedures and resourcing. They plan teaching activities and assessments to give students the opportunity to achieve the objectives of the National Curriculum. Students work with activities and resources provided by teachers to achieve learning objectives.	Students demonstrate their achievements and give feedback to the teacher about their learning needs. How can students give better feedback to teachers? What skills do they need? What information do they need about the curriculum and what is expected of them?
Students	

Diagram 2

Activity

Make a blank chart with the same layout as Diagram 2. Enter onto it the requirements and responsibilities, and the accountability and feedback mechanisms applicable in your school. Include such things as the annual appraisal by the Board of Trustees of the Principal's performance, job descriptions, individual education programmes for students, the school policy on assessment, and procedures for filling out attendance registers. Add items you listed in the first two activities. Read *School Charters and the Revised National Educational Guidelines* to find other requirements. In particular note the implications of the first of the 'National Administration Guidelines' within that statement.

Discuss the systems you have seen operating in other schools. For example, is staff input sought during the annual appraisal of the Principal?

Diagram 3 shows the same chain of responsibility as Diagram 2 but this time it is turned on its side. The loops around each group of people represent planning loops like the one in Diagram 1. This shows that each group and individual in the chain has a planning responsibility. The arrows show that each group has a responsibility to be influenced by the achievements and needs of others in the chain, and each has a responsibility to pass on information about their own achievements and needs to others, as in Diagram 2. Notice the place of the Education Review Office. It is not part of the chain for a particular school. It does not advise or offer additional support to schools. Its function is to monitor and observe whether the chain of responsibility described above is operating effectively.

Before and After 1989

In the education system which operated prior to 1989 there was an additional layer of people between the school and the government. Inspectors had a role as monitors of the system. They had some discretionary power to allocate additional resources where they identified special needs. They also had power to inform the politicians about particular needs they observed in schools and classrooms. That flow of information is not there any more. It is replaced by the flow of information within the school system.

The inspectorate was part of a different structure; one where boards, managers, teachers and learners had less responsibility and autonomy than they have under the current system. The inspectors made judgements about how the curriculum should be taught and advised schools and teachers about how to improve. In general these were wise, benevolent people who had a good understanding of teaching and learning, and they had expertise in their subject areas.

Responsibilities in the New Zealand Education System

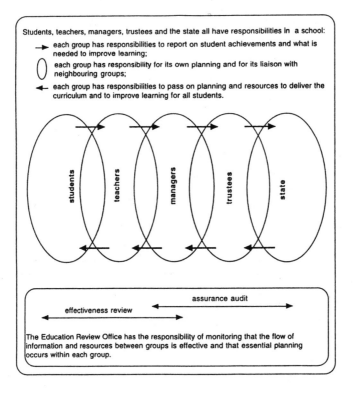

Students, teachers, managers, trustees and the state all have responsibilities in a school:

- each group has responsibilities to report on student achievements and what is needed to improve learning;

- each group has responsibility for its own planning and for its liaison with neighbouring groups;

- each group has responsibilities to pass on planning and resources to deliver the curriculum and to improve learning for all students.

students   teachers   managers   trustees   state

assurance audit
effectiveness review

The Education Review Office has the responsibility of monitoring that the flow of information and resources between groups is effective and that essential planning occurs within each group.

Diagram 3

Under today's system boards, managers, teachers and students all have responsibilities for their links in the learning cycle. They each have responsibility to ensure that the national curriculum is taught and learned and that the resources allocated to them are used well. They each have responsibility to feed back information about needs and achievements. If schools lack the expertise to be sure they are meeting the expectations of the curriculum, or addressing student needs, they are expected to take the initiative to rectify the situation, perhaps by consulting with experts from outside the school.

There are two ways in which the new system breaks down within a school. Firstly if policies, procedures, and expectations are not clearly specified then teachers and students are unable to operate independently within prescribed boundaries. The second problem, which relates to the flow of information on the right-hand side of Diagram 2, has already been discussed. It is a more common problem, partly because many educators are used to the more authoritarian system of the past where their routine work was supervised by others.

Many people argue that our current system is better because it gives more opportunities for people to be independent and follow their own talents and interests within the boundaries set down. It encourages people to be responsible and it encourages learners to be independent and use their initiative. Other people mourn the loss of a benevolent system of supervision which brought advice, guidance and support to teachers, regardless of whether it was asked for. It allowed more direct pressure to be applied to the government for resources and funding for education, and more direct feedback to government about pressures in the system.

Whether we like the current system or not, it is one which will operate effectively only if each person in the system analyses needs and takes the initiative to find ways of addressing those needs. This is our challenge for the future.

References

Caldwell, B and Spinks, J M. (1988). *The Self-Managing School.* Falmer Press.

Mathematics in the New Zealand Curriculum. (1992). Ministry of Education.

School Charters and the Revised National Educational Guidelines. Education Gazette, 30 April 1993 pp3-4.

Principal's Implementation Task Force. (1990). *A Guide to the Delivery of Educational Objectives.* Ministry of Education.

Principal's Implementation Task Force. (1990). *A Guide to Governance and Management.* Ministry of Education.

Stewart, D and Prebble, T. (1985). *Making it Happen: a School Development Process.* Dunmore Press.

9   Planning in Mathematics

Liz Stone, Geoff Woolford, Kerry Taylor and Ray Wilson

Introduction

Who or what decides the content of your mathematics programme and
the way you teach it? Is it you? The National Curriculum? Your head
of department or syndicate leader? The nature of the resources you
commonly use? Or a mixture of these and other factors? Diagram 1
highlights the many factors that influence teachers, directly or
indirectly, when they are planning and teaching a programme.

Discussion
Look at Diagram 1. How does each factor influence a mathematics
programme, and how important do you think each factor is? Show
the relative importance of each factor by the thickness of the arrow
you draw from it, into the central question.

Diagram 2 shows how these factors can be summarized and the effect
that they all might have on long-term and short-term planning.
   When planning a lesson or unit of work, some teachers start with
a collection of mathematics activities which they know to be 'rich'
(see Chapter 11 in Volume 1) and then decide which learning
objectives are covered by these activities. Others plan in the opposite
way: they decide what their learning objectives are going to be and
then look around for rich mathematical activities which support them.
Most teachers probably do a little bit of both and would find themselves somewhere between the two ends on the following continuum

Start with rich mathemat- ———————————— Start with learning objec-
ical activities, then identify   tives, then find suitable rich
learning objectives.   mathematical activities.

Where do you fit on this continuum? Do you feel more comfortable
starting with a problem or investigation and working from there? Or
do you prefer to start with a couple of objectives from the curriculum?

J. Neyland (ed), Mathematics Education: A Handbook for Teachers, Vol.2, 86-93
© *1995 Wellington College of Education: New Zealand*

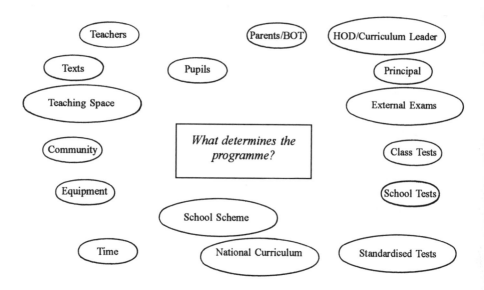

Diagram 1

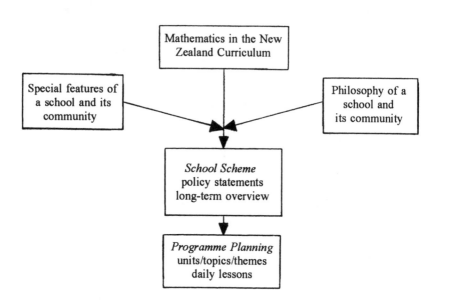

Diagram 2

Stone et al.

Long-Term Planning

Teachers need to plan an overview for the year to ensure that they will be giving adequate coverage to all the content strands of the curriculum. Often the overview is provided by the maths resource teacher or head of department as part of the scheme. If you ever need to plan your own it is useful to be aware of the range of options available to you. We shall outline four common approaches.

1. The Topic Approach
This approach focuses directly on the mathematical content to be learned, and has many forms.

(i) Some teachers prefer to use a small number of *broad topic headings*, for example, 'Number'. They choose the learning objectives connected with this topic bearing in mind the individual learning needs of the students in their class. A broad topic approach gives them the flexibility to meet individual needs and to take a more holistic approach to their teaching.
(ii) Alternatively, some topic approaches break mathematics into a *large number of small units*, for example, 'Number' might be divided into 'Whole Numbers', 'Factors and Primes', 'Integers', and 'Fractions'. This gives strong guidance to a teacher, but if taken literally, each unit includes only a small number of learning objectives and that rarely suits the range of needs in the usual classroom. A number of small topics such as this can make it difficult for pupils to see how the ideas relate to each other and connect with other topics.

So which approach is better? Perhaps it depends on the teacher's own knowledge and confidence. The fewer the topics the greater the flexibility and opportunity to make links across ideas. The larger the number of topics the greater the specific guidance for the inexperienced teacher, but the more constrained the learning experiences for the students.

2. The Cyclic Approach
In this approach a topic is revisited several times during the year in a cycle. Each time a topic comes up in the cycle the students build upon the learning in the previous cycle. Beginning School Mathematics is an example of a programme that uses the cyclic approach.

3. The Thematic Approach

Unlike the previous two approaches, when there is usually little input from students into the planning process, the *thematic* approach can develop from events of high interest to the pupils, for example, the Rugby World Cup. The students may choose the theme themselves, or choose which aspect of a theme they would like to explore. Here is an example of a thematic unit from Te Wharekura O Hoani Waititi where the third form students explore the mathematics involved when they organise a hui.

Te Whakahaere Hui   (Organizing a Hui)
- How do we find out what is the best buy in the supermarket?
- Budgeting
- Catering
- Travel: costs, distances
- Using past histories to help us

Thematic units also lend themselves easily to cross-curricular studies. For example, a class studying pollution in science can also look at the mathematics of measurement. A further advantage of a thematic approach is that it makes use of resources from the world of the student, thus increasing the chance of student interest and involvement in the mathematics programme. Some teachers worry that they will not cover the required content when using a thematic approach. Teachers using this approach, then, need to clearly focus on, and make explicit, the mathematics learned (and maintained) during the theme. They need to be explicit in their planning, and they need to help the students be clear about the mathematics they are learning. They will then be able to identify achievement objectives that require further learning, and build them into future themes or topics.

Discussion
What approaches have you seen used in the schools you have visited?
What do you see are the advantages and disadvantages of each approach?
Which approach do you feel most comfortable with?

4. Topic Approach with Cycles and Themes

The three approaches mentioned above are not mutually exclusive. There can be merit in combining them to capitalise on their strengths and minimising their weaknesses. One common way of combining all three is illustrated by the following example showing the first six weeks of a term's programme.

One Term Overview		
Week	*Main Focus*	*Maintenance*
1	Theme: Summer Sports	Number
2	Geometry	Statistics
3	Theme: Myself	Geometry
4	Number	Algebra
5	Measurement	Number
6	Geometry	Measurement

Short-Term Planning

The long-term plan provides the overview for the term or year. But what are the students actually going to do? How will you blend together the process and content objectives? Which learning experiences will you use? How will you know whether the students are learning anything? How will you know if your programme is working? As part of your short-term planning you will need to answer all of these questions.

Let's discuss two of these questions further. How do you blend together process and content objectives, and how do you choose your learning experiences? The simplest way is to choose *rich mathematical activities* as the basis of all your learning units. If an activity is 'rich' it will automatically involve the use of the process objectives. Many teachers use a table like Table 1 to help them sort out the activities they will use for a unit.

PLANNING 'RICH' MATHEMATICAL ACTIVITIES FOR:	Form 2 Shape							
	FAVOURITE ACTIVITIES							
ACHIEVEMENT OUTCOMES	Building Polygons	LOGO	Circle Designs	Treasure Hunt	Kowhaiwhai	4-bit houses		
Processes								
Problem Solving	✓	✓	✓	✓	✓	✓		
Logic and Reasoning		✓			✓	✓		
Communication			✓	✓	✓			
Content								
Construct Triangle, Circle	✓		✓					
Nets of Polygons								
Plan Views						✓		
Location/Bearings				✓				
Symmetry Polygons		✓			✓			
Rotation		✓			✓			
Enlarge 2-D		✓						

Table 1

They use steps similar to these.

Step 1: They list the specific content objectives they wish to cover in this topic (e.g., 'construct a triangle').

Step 2: They then make a list of the mathematical activities they already know about which have links with the topic, or they search through resource books for ideas.

Step 3: This step involves a bit of analysis of the chosen activities by ticking the appropriate boxes beneath them on the table. If an activity does not have a tick against at least one of the process objectives, another one is sought to replace it.

Step 4:   Are there other mathematical skills the activities cover?
           These are noted on the remaining blank lines on the table,
           and become part of the maintenance programme.
Step 5:   If two activities cover the same objectives, one might be
           used for introduction and the other for maintenance or
           assessment.

Discussion
What short-term planning models have you seen when visiting
schools?
How did the teachers select the activities to ensure mathematical
processes were included as well as content?
How did the teachers select the activities to ensure a balanced
mathematics programme, with the learning of new concepts and
maintenance of skills?

Establishing Daily Routines

The daily organisation of the mathematics session is achieved by using
routines which ensure that time is given to do all the tasks that make
up a balanced learning programme.

Many teachers use small groups of pupils on a three to five day
rotation of activities to ensure all of them experience all the activities.
Others allocate separate days for new learning activities and for
maintenance work. Still others, by choosing very rich mathematical
activities, ensure that maintenance of skills is built into their everyday
programme. Whatever organisation is adopted, time must be allocated
for the following:

- introduction of new concepts;
- practice of ideas just learned and the maintenance of previous
  learning;
- enrichment experiences that broaden ideas and have intrinsic
  appeal to the pupils;
- "choice time" - an opportunity for pupils to select maths tasks for
  their own purposes, thus building personal responsibility and
  commitment to doing mathematics for its own sake;
- ongoing assessment of learning;
- reflection time - for programme evaluation and for pupil self-
  assessment.

Discussion

How do teachers, through their daily routines, ensure that all pupils have an opportunity to experience the full balance of learning activities?

How do you organise a lesson so that the students can interact with each other, and so that the teacher can interact with the students?

Summary

When planning a teaching and learning programme, the teacher needs to:

1. Establish the aims of the programme from national, local and personal perspectives.
2. Establish a long-term plan that ensures adequate coverage of all the strands of the curriculum.
3. Develop a short-term plan that includes rich mathematical activities. The short-term plan will also need to state the resources and the assessment procedures that will be used.
4. Plan a management model that will ensure that all pupils experience a range of learning activities.

Initially the tasks will seem huge! But make sure you seek support from the teacher-in-charge of mathematics at your school. As it says in *Better Mathematics*:

A scheme cannot be a substitute for an ongoing dialogue with colleagues. This generates more ideas and increased awareness of pupils' needs. The continuing process of development is more important than the particular details of the curriculum. There is no short-cut and this takes time.

(Better Mathematics, p.54)

Reference

Ahmed, A (1987) *Better Mathematics* West Sussex Institute of Higher Education, Upper Bognor Rd, Bognor Regis, West Sussex, UK.

10   Assessment of Girls

Thora Blithe, Megan Clark and Sharleen Forbes

Discussion Questions

- What are the purposes of mathematics assessment in: early childhood, primary, secondary and tertiary education?
- What attitudes, skills, knowledge and understanding do we want to assess in mathematics?
- What is fair assessment in mathematics?
- Does having the same assessment for everyone ensure fairness?
- Which types of assessment in mathematics favour boys? What are the reasons for this?
- Should the assessment of girls be any different from that of boys? Why?

Introduction

Children are constantly assessed throughout their schooling. This assessment may be diagnostic, to identify a child's strengths or weaknesses or where the child is 'at'. It may be formative, so a teacher can sensibly plan an appropriate programme for a child. It may be summative, to sum up a child's achievements and progress and to inform parents, caregivers, prospective employers or higher reaches of the school system. In the last years of secondary school, assessment is also used for the award of formal qualifications. Assessment therefore has enormous potential for enrichment or harm in a child's life.

We usually assume that the various tests and assessment tools that we use measure what we think they measure (are reliable). But they don't always. A lovely example of Marilyn Yeoman's, is a picture of three birds and two worms shown to new entrants. They were asked the question: "How many birds don't get a worm?" You can see what the question is trying to find out. But all sorts of confident (and correct) answers emerged, for example, "all of them, the worms were too quick"! It's easy to see the problem here. But it's not so easy when we get to School Certificate and other important exams. In fact, there is a growing concern that often they are not reliable.

We take it for granted that assessment should be fair. But what do we mean by fair? Does it mean giving everyone the same test under the same conditions? Does it mean giving everyone a fair chance to demonstrate their individual skills? How can we do that?

Some types of assessment unfairly advantage one group of students over another. According to *Tomorrows Standards* (1990) "assessment is never neutral." Certainly many traditional forms of assessment in mathematics disadvantage girls. These days both teaching and assessment have to be suitable for the broader range of students now taking mathematics. Typically girls and boys view mathematics achievement differently. Girls habitually attribute their successes to hard work or luck rather than ability and their failures to a lack of ability, whereas boys view it the other way around (Barnes et al., 1987). As girls go on in mathematics they have a decreased expectation of success. We need to convince girls of their own abilities and help them to acquire greater confidence. We have to tell our good female pupils that they are good, and encourage them to go on with further study.

Gender Differences in Assessment

In the United States, Britain and New Zealand the performance of women in traditional mathematics examinations has been poor compared to that of men, both in participation and in achievement. However, we don't see these gender differences in all cultures (Hanna, 1988). Women cannot be classified as a single group. Forbes (1992) showed that in some assessment situations Maori and Pakeha girls perform differently. Jenny Young-Loveridge (1992) in her work with junior and middle primary school children suggests that when comparing girls and boys, socio-economic status and ethnicity should be taken into consideration and that looking at gender alone is liable to be misleading.

Is it appropriate to have assessment procedures consistently designed by one minority section of the population (in the case of mathematics, by Pakeha men) applied to the whole population? Wouldn't it be fairer and more informative to use a variety of methods to assess a student's attainment, rather than to rely on a single three-hour performance to indicate the outcome of, in some cases, several years of study?

In the seventh form Bursary exam, girls in both co-educational and single-sex schools usually perform less well than boys. But these differences are not consistent across school authorities (state, integrated and private schools). Different sorts of schools have different sorts of students (and different sorts of girls), which reinforces the view that girls cannot be seen as one homogeneous group. But, it's important to remember that all research results indicate a greater range of mathematical achievement within each gender than between the genders. Can you explain what this means?

Assessment Practices

In School Certificate in past years subjects were ranked. The higher a subject was ranked, the more students passed that subject. Traditionally 'male' subjects are near the top of the rankings, while traditionally 'female' subjects are near the bottom. There are a number of School Certificate subjects in which over three-quarters of the candidates are male, and a number in which over three-quarters of the candidates are female. Of those dominated by boys there were three (Chemistry, Physical Sciences and Physics) in 1989 where almost a third of the class received A grades (Ministry of Education, 1990). This didn't happen in any of the subjects like Typing or Home Economics dominated by girls. Does this indicate that 'boys' subjects are valued more than the 'girls' ones? Sixth Form Certificate is moderated by a school's School Certificate performance and so "the gender bias will be carried like pollen on the backs of the grades allocated to the school" (McDonald, 1992). Bursary examination scores are also based on a subject hierarchy, with the subjects traditionally taken by males dominating the hierarchy. In 1989 the Universities Entrance Board (cited in McDonald, 1992), stated that " . . . the large majority of scholarships are gained by students who enter two of their three scholarship papers in Chemistry, Mathematics with Calculus, Mathematics with Statistics, or Physics." Unsurprisingly this resulted in a majority of scholarships going to males.

Some secondary schools use the practice of making the students' test results fit a 'normal' curve in the mistaken belief that this is how the scores ought to fall. This is particularly inappropriate with small classes. A worrying trend is the use of results in national examinations as a measure not only of students' performance but also of the teacher's or the school's performance. Although it might be true that 'a bad doctor only loses one patient, but a bad teacher destroys hundreds' we must be extremely careful not to use inappropriate measures to evaluate teacher performance. We know very little about the interaction between 'good' and 'bad' teachers and students' performance on tests. When students' marks are used to assess teachers or schools this is usually done without taking into account different intakes of students, or the "value-added" component of the assessment (that is, the improvement in the student's knowledge). In the 'Mathematics for All?' study (Forbes et al., 1990) when the performance of third-formers was compared at the beginning and end of the year using the same mathematics test, one of the lowest-scoring classes at both the beginning and end of the year had one of the highest gains during the year. In other words, the class learned a great deal. This class was in a small rural school, all the students were Maori and the majority were girls. It is likely that the critical factor in the class improvement was the young enthusiastic Maori mathematics/science specialist who was their teacher. If the students' end of year scores had been used as an indicator of this teacher's performance it would have been quite an unfair and incorrect assessment of his efforts.

Types of Assessment

There are many forms of assessment in current use in mathematics. These include:
- timed/speed tests (where problems need to be solved within a set period of time),
- multi-choice tests (where students chose from either yes/no, true/false, or a range of options),
- written essays and reports,
- oral presentations,
- individual projects (usually done over a period of days or weeks),
- group projects,
- mastery learning (where basic facts at one level have to be "mastered" before progressing to the next level),
- two or three hour written examinations, and
- internal assessment (generally done by teachers throughout the course and often involving a combination of some or all of the above methods, including teacher observation).

Although most national secondary school examinations in mathematics in New Zealand are three hour written examinations, there is now an internally assessed (but nationally moderated) option for School Certificate. Sixth Form Certificate is internally assessed within each school (but nationally moderated on the school's previous years School Certificate performance over all subjects), and a portion (20%) of the Bursary Mathematics with Statistics paper is internally assessed (but nationally moderated on the school's Bursary examination performance).

Timed Tests. Girls often perform better on tests which are not timed. Eliminating time restrictions can improve female performance (Rosser, 1989). The Ministry of Education (1992) acknowledges that traditional time-constrained pencil and paper tests have proved unreliable indicators of Maori achievement in the past. While we don't suggest that fixed-time tests shouldn't be used, it is probably fairer to use them in conjunction with other assessment tools.

Multiple-choice questions. Boys are favoured by multiple-choice questions (Willis, 1990). Males are more likely than females to guess answers to multiple-choice questions and this may be a cause of differences in performance. If girls don't know the correct option they are more likely than boys to leave the question out rather than guess. Women are also more likely to select the "I don't know" option when it is available (Wilder and Powell, 1989). This tendency for women to be 'less likely to gamble' might be reduced if penalties are not given for wrong answers. In situations where students are required to guess answers to questions they would normally leave out, girls guess correctly more often than boys. Girls are more likely than boys to stop when they meet difficulties and not to work completely through questions they find hard. It seems that girls are less willing to take risks in mathematics and so are disadvantaged by multiple-choice assessment and especially by negative marking schemes. A secondary objection to multiple-choice questions is that they reinforce the right/wrong image of mathematics which puts off many pupils.

Essay questions. Girls perform better than boys on essay-type questions (Willis, 1990; Assessment and Gender, 1992). In the 1987 and 1988 Bursary mathematics papers one of only two questions where girls did significantly better than boys, was an essay question (Forbes et al., 1990). Essay-type questions provide an opportunity to elaborate on an issue, to show understanding, to exercise judgement, and to consider a range of possibilities. Unfortunately, students who shine in these areas often find themselves limited by the time restrictions.

Other assessment modes. Girls may perform more or less the same as boys on oral tasks or take-home tasks (for example in the Netherlands, de Lange, 1987). Megan Clark (1989) suggests that the introduction of comprehension (of mathematical material) questions (as in SMP, A levels) might be useful. An advantage is that pupils get to read some mathematics and the most usual way engineers, psychologists, geographers, etc., meet mathematics is when they need to read someone else's work and understand it. The preparation for such a question encourages group discussion and encourages a social element to teaching - all 'girl-friendly' stuff.

Content and Context of Test Questions

In New Zealand (Forbes et al., 1990) when students are offered a choice of questions in mathematics examinations the selections of boys and girls can often be quite different. It is likely that both the content and the context of questions influence question selection.

The small but consistent gender differences in achievement that we see may only reflect biases in the type of test used and the content of the test. Girls' mathematics achievement is measured by the assessment of their performance in the intended curriculum, although the curriculum is itself gender-biased in favour of males (Leahy, 1992). Leahy points out that girls can be disadvantaged in mathematics when they get rewarded for, stereotyped 'feminine' behaviour which encourages rote-learning and rule following rather than experimentation, problem solving and risk-taking.

Content. In the United Kingdom (Girls and Mathematics, 1986), a number of differences between the mathematical performance of boys and girls have been found:
* at primary school girls and boys achieved the same overall but differences occur in specific topics;
* the one area in which girls perform significantly better than boys at primary level (computation) decreases in importance for the study of mathematics at secondary school;
* boys, by the end of their primary schooling, appear to have developed the problem-solving, risk taking approach to learning mathematics needed to succeed at secondary school level;
* the top 30% of achievers accounted for most of the gender differences in performance at ages 11 and 15;
* in secondary school surveys, the boys average scores were higher than the girls in every category, with the exception of modern algebra.

Females tend to perform best in the areas of knowledge and skills, and they outperform males on tasks which require rule-following. Males are advantaged by items which require problem-solving techniques or an application of mathematics. Females shine in explicitly described computational tasks and don't do as well in word problems requiring problem-solving techniques. Tests with mixed mathematical content favour males. Some research indicates that gender differences increase in favour of boys as the level of complexity of an item increases (Fennema, 1974). Generally, gender differences increase in favour of boys as we move from arithmetic to algebra to geometry. It has been suggested by Kimball (1993) that this is possibly the reason that arithmetic is considered less important than problem solving. That is, we value problem solving because boys are good at it and we undervalue computational skills because it is something girls do well. What do you think of this idea? What mathematics skills do we need most in life?

In general terms. Girls do well in areas (computation, logic, algebra) where content bias towards boys' interests or experiences is least likely to occur (Chipman, 1981). Gender differences tend not to appear when tests cover subject matter which is almost exclusively taught and learned in the classroom. In New Zealand, Wily (1986) has confirmed most of these findings and, in particular:
- boys achieve better than girls on questions which require mathematical reasoning, an understanding of spatial concepts and visualisation, and applied mathematics;
- with questions which require two or more steps, usually more girls than boys work through part of the question correctly and then fail to complete it; and
- girls tend to perform as well, or better than, boys in questions on calculus or complex numbers.

Context. There are at least three kinds of context bias in questions: quantity bias (the number of males and females referred to in a question); stereotype bias (the roles in which each gender is portrayed); and status bias (the relative status at which each gender is portrayed).

Word problems are usually set in the context of life situations, which may vary in familiarity for males and females. This is a likely source of gender differences. Females achieve better on items with 'feminine' or 'gender' neutral content. (e.g., Rosser, 1989; Clark, 1993). Graf and Riddell (1972) found that it took females longer to solve a problem set in a stock market than it took them to solve an identical problem set in the context of buying goods in a fabric store i.e., the context can affect the speed of solution. Many tests refer to males more than females, portray males in higher status positions, and use stereotyped gender roles. Mathematics questions using 'male' vocabulary may well have a negative effect on the performance of females. In seventh form statistics questions little difference has been seen in male and female performance. Can you suggest why this is so?

Test Administration

The way in which a test is administered can affect performance and gender differences (Willis, 1990). Achievement is often higher in a many problem mathematics test when the items are presented singly than when they are presented together as a test, and this improvement is greater for girls. Young-Loveridge (1992) suggests that the traditional use of written mathematics tests advantages children with better literacy skills. It is possible that the lack of gender differences in number achievement at the primary school level may be due to differences in literacy (which favour girls) cancelling out differences in mathematics which favour boys.

Leahy (1992) recommends that self-assessment programmes should be used very carefully given the differences in boys and girls perceptions of their own abilities. In New Zealand girls tend to perform less well and make less effort in competitive situations when they think their performance is being judged. Leahy recommends the routine use of 'blind marking' (where the identity of the student is not known) to eliminate any marker bias towards boys.

Confidence and Competitiveness

The common view of mathematics as 'masculine' means that males and females have different attitudes to achievement. Males are more likely to expect success than females, as they tend to explain their failures as being caused by external factors like luck and lack of effort while their successes are seen as due to their own ability. Girls express greater uncertainty than boys about their mathematical performance at all ability levels and attribute their failures to lack of ability. Boys tend to over-rate their performance whereas girls tend to under-rate (Willis, 1990). Girls are less confident than boys about continued achievement.

Amount of Mathematics Studied

A partial explanation for gender differences in mathematics performance in the senior secondary school is that females tend to take less mathematics than males. In the eighties in the seventh form in New Zealand, more boys than girls took Applied Mathematics and Physics, as well as Mathematics, and in this way gained a broader understanding of mathematical concepts, as well as extra practice in techniques (Wily, 1986). A smaller percentage of girls than boys take both of the Bursary mathematics papers currently offered (Forbes et al., 1990).

Forbes et al. concluded that "the higher proportion of girls opting to do only one paper is probably the largest contributing factor to the apparent gender differences in performance." According to Fennema (1979) the single most important influence on learning mathematics is studying mathematics. Frequently males do more mathematics than females in senior secondary school so it's not surprising they do better.

Examinations or Internal Assessment?

It's widely believed that girls are likely to perform better, when using internal assessment rather than external timed examinations. An alarming development in Britain is that when a component of internal assessment was introduced and girls did then perform better, after a short period of time the internally assessed component was substantially reduced (Burton, 1993).

People worry about how to fairly administer internally assessed components of qualifications and often assume that cheating is more common with internal assessment. But we have no idea what the current level of cheating in public examinations is and it may well be that cheating is just more visible in internal assessment. This question of timed exam versus non-timed assessment work has major implications for secondary schools with their emphasis on School Certificate, Sixth Form Certificate and Bursary. In New Zealand primary schools, with the increasing use of various national and Australian competitive tests, the issue is assuming greater importance than in the past. In the fifth-form the three-hour end-of-year written examination, School Certificate, is used to assess mathematics performance. In the sixth form, however, the internally assessed (using a variety of means including tests and projects) Sixth Form Certificate is used. But the Sixth Form Certificate grades available for schools to allocate to students are fixed by the school's overall performance in the previous year's School Certificate (that is, Sixth Form Certificate is moderated by School Certificate). Does that seem sensible or fair?

In School Certificate a higher percentage of boys than girls scored in the top three grades, but in Sixth Form Certificate only in the very highest grade did boys do better than girls which may indicate that the girls perform better with internal assessment.

(i) Sixth form grades in Mathematics. More males obtain the very high and very low grades, and females dominate in the middle grades. This is also a familiar pattern in some European countries (Burton, 1993). However, the proportion of females who do really well (A1) in School Certificate mathematics and then go on to obtain a 1 in sixth form

certificate mathematics is higher than that of males. So, there is some evidence that internal assessment of mathematics reduces the gender difference in the top scores that we see with timed exams.

(ii) Bursary. In the 1988 Mathematics with Statistics bursary exam 20% of the final overall mark was obtained from an internally assessed "project" component, and 80% from a national end of year three-hour written examination. There was a small but significant gender difference in overall performance in favour of the boys. But, on average girls had a higher placing within their school on the project than on the examination, and boys had a higher placing on the examination than the project, (that is, if a girl was third in her school on project marks she might be seventh in the exam).

So girls did seem to do better in the internally assessed component than in the examination. But it's a statistics exam. Many practising statisticians would hold the view that it is exactly the research, problem-solving and report-writing skills tested in the internal assessment that are essential; not the ability to regurgitate or manipulate standard formulae in a set time. Should the project be given equal weighting with the written examination? Certainly the practice of moderating the project mark by the examination marks needs urgent review - can it possibly be justified?

(iii) University. At university in New Zealand there are also indications that females perform better in statistics when they are internally assessed, rather than when they sit traditional single three-hour end-of-year examinations. In a module based internally assessed mathematics course, females are more likely to complete all modules than boys and do better in this part of the course. Would it be fairer if all our assessment for formal qualifications was a mixture of these two types of assessment?

Order and Choice in Tests and Examinations

Mathematics examinations often offer students a choice of questions especially in national examinations. The choice is offered in order to make the examination "fair" for all students. But if males and females are choosing different questions is this fair? How do we ensure that the different questions have the same level of difficulty?

In past Bursary and Scholarship mathematics papers there have been significant differences between the selections of male and female students. Bursary and Scholarships Mathematics with Statistics papers contain both mathematics and statistics questions. Girls have shown

(Forbes et al., 1990) a marked preference for the statistics questions. This could be because considerably fewer girls than boys take both mathematics papers in the seventh form and there is substantial overlap between Mathematics with Calculus and the mathematics section of Mathematics with Statistics. There is also a slight tendency for both boys and girls to score better on questions they answered early in the examination. At least a quarter of all students answer their chosen questions in exactly the order they appear in the paper (that is, all the mathematics questions followed by all the statistics questions). This is slightly less marked for girls than boys even though more girls choose a statistics question as their final option. It is possible that the order of the sections in this examination unfairly disadvantage girls.

No one has paid much attention to the order in which either questions, or sections of questions, appear in examination papers. As this order may influence the order in which students answer questions, we can't dismiss it as unimportant. We need to be sure that order itself does not unfairly disadvantage any group of students.

Some first year university results can be applied to schools. In a statistics service course in which females invariably outperform males, performance is best in questions about 'people' or 'the environment'. When given a choice of questions with identical content women in this course were more likely to take a second option with a 'people' context if the first was set in some stereotypically 'masculine' context such as 'concrete'. Questions with particular contexts will allow different groups of students to shine.

Summary

There is a considerable body of evidence to suggest that girls are advantaged by internal assessment procedures. Thee often test different skills than mathematics examinations, and the use of examination results to either moderate or 'out-weigh' the internal assessment can't be justified. While males still outperform females on mathematics tests, the gap between the sexes appears to be slowly narrowing (with the exception of very high levels of achievement) and latest indications from Bursary are that the gap has virtually disappeared. The following have been shown to disadvantage girls in some assessment situations: timed tests, multi-choice tests, question content (area of mathematics), question context (real-life situation in which the question is embedded), and order of examination or test questions. However, girls perform better or the same as boys on essays, oral tasks or take-home tasks. The higher the proportion of course work, the better females achieve(in the United Kingdom, Burton, 1993). Changes in learning and assessing styles can lead to improvements in the performance of females.

No single form of assessment will be equally fair for both boys and girls. This is particularly true when the style, content and context of test questions are also considered. We can't look at these aspects of examinations as being objective. They are gender and culturally specific and, in general, reflect the world of the mathematics examiners. You should carefully examine all aspects of your assessment practices to ensure that girls are not disproportionately disadvantaged.

The areas in which girls succeed well (computation and algebra) become less important in senior secondary school whereas the areas boys succeed in (geometry and problem-solving) become more useful for higher level mathematics. Girls are less confident of success in mathematics than boys, and appear to take less risks; omitting rather than guessing answers. When girls are successful they are likely to attribute it to luck, whereas boys attribute success to talent. Girls generally do better in statistics rather than mathematics questions. While the number of mathematics papers being studied is a major influence on mathematics performance in secondary school this isn't the case at university level where there is less overlap in content between papers. Girls prefer questions set in 'environmental' or 'people' contexts and do better on familiar or standard rather than problem-solving questions. Girls perform well in essay-type questions, and are advantaged by internal assessment procedures rather than examinations.

Within the broad group of females are sub-groups (Maori women, poor women, etc.) with particular needs. Research into particular groups of women and how assessment affects them is urgently needed. In order for assessment to promote and encourage further learning, rather than reinforce failure or be a barrier to progress, students need to see assessment as 'fair'. It would be fairer and more informative to use a variety of procedures to assess student's mathematics performance.

Society's mathematical needs have both increased and changed dramatically in recent years. The need is not just for mathematical knowledge but also for the ability to use that knowledge in a wide range of areas, and to be able to communicate that knowledge.

Further Reading

Burton, L. (ed.) (1986). *Girls Into Mathematics Can Go*, Holt, Rinehart and Winston.

EQUALS. (1989). *Assessment Alternatives in Mathematics*. Lawrence

Hall of Science. University of California at Berkeley. USA.

Forbes, Sharleen, Blithe, Thora, Clark, Megan, and Robinson, Elizabeth, (1990). *Mathematics for all? Summary of a study of participation, performance, gender and ethnic differences in mathematics,* Ministry of Education, Wellington.

Forbes, Sharleen and Mako, Cyril (1993). *Assessment in Education : A Diagnostic Tool or a Barrier to Progress.* Paper to be presented to the 1993 World Indigenous Peoples Conference: Education. Woolongong, Australia.

Girls and Mathematics, (1986). A report by the joint Mathematical Education Committee of The Royal Society and The Institute of Mathematics and its Applications, London.

Irving, James, (1991). *Current Developments in Educational Assessment,* Paper presented at the Annual Combined Meeting of the Manawatu and Wanganui Principals' Associations, Palmerston North, New Zealand.

Te Puni Kokiri, (1993). *Pangarau - Maori Mathematics and Education.* Te Puni Kokiri (Ministry of Maori Development), Wellington, New Zealand.

Walden, Rosie and Walkerdine, Valerie, (1985). *Girls and Mathematics from Primary to Secondary Schooling,* Institute of Education, University of London, England.

References

Assessment and Gender, (1992). Girls and Womens Section, Policy Division, Ministry of Education. Background paper for the National Workshop on Professional Development in Educational Assessment, Educational Assessment Secretariat, Ministry of Education, Wellington, New Zealand.

Barnes, M. Plaister, R. and Thomas, A (1987). *Girls Count in Mathematics and Science.* Reprinted. Education Department of Western Australia.

Burton, L. (1993). *Differential Performance in Assessment in Mathematics at the end of Compulsory Schooling.* Paper delivered to 'Symposium on International Comparisons and National Evaluation Methods' at the Fifth Conference of the European Association for Research on Learning and Instruction. Aix-en-Provence. August 31-September 5.

Chipman, Susan, (1988). *Word Problems: Where Test Bias Creeps In,* Paper presented at the Annual Meeting of the American Educational Research Association, New Orleans, LA.

Clark, Megan, (1989). Examinations for All. *New Zealand Mathemat-*

ics Magazine, Vol 26, No.1, pp22-25.

Clark, Megan, (1993). Friend or Foe? The pressure for change. *New Zealand Journal of Mathematics.* Vol 22, pp29-42.

de Lange. J. (1987). *Mathematics, Insight and Meaning.* Utrecht: OW & OC.

Fennema, E. (1979). Women and Girls in Mathematics - Equity in Mathematics Education, *Educational Studies in Mathematics,* Vol 10, pp389-401.

Fennema, E. (1974). Sex Differences in Mathematics Learning: Why??, *The Elementary School Journal,* Vol 75, pp183-190.

Forbes, Sharleen, (1992). *Age 13: Mathematics and me for the New Zealand Maori girl,* Paper presented to the Seventh International Conference on Mathematics Education.

Graf, F., and Riddell, J. (1992). Sex Differences in Problem-solving as a Function of Problem Context. *The Journal of Educational Research,* Vol 65, No.10.

Hanna, Gila, (1988). *Girls and Boys About Equal in Mathematics Achievement in Eighth Grade Results from Twenty Countries,* The Ontario Institute for Studies in Education. Paper presented at the Sixth International Congress on Mathematical Education, Budapest, Hungary. Kimball, M. (1993). Contribution to panel discussion at ICMI Study 93 Gender and Mathematics.

Leahy, Helen (1992). *How assessment procedures can take into account and reflect the specific needs, values, and concepts of girls and women,* Girls and Women section, Ministry of Education, Wellington, New Zealand.

McDonald, Geraldine (1992). 'Are Girls Smarter than Boys?' in S. Middleton and A. Jones (eds), *Women and Education in Aotearoa II,* Bridget Williams Books, New Zealand.

Ministry of Education, (1990). *1989 New Zealand School Certificate and Sixth Form Certificate Statistics.* Research and Statistics Division. Ministry of Education. Wellington.

Ministry of Education, (1992). *Mathematics in the New Zealand Curriculum: Draft,* Learning Media, Ministry of Education, Wellington.

Purser, P.M., and Wily, H.M. (1992). *What turns them on: An investigation of motivation in the responses of students to mathe-matics questions,* Burnside High School, Christchurch, New Zealand.

Rosser, Phyllis, (1989). *The SAT gender gap: identifying the causes.* Centre for Policy Studies, Washington DC.

Tomorrows Standards, (1990). Report of the Ministerial Working Party on Assessment for Better Learning. Learning Media, Wellington.

Wilder, Gita Z. and Powell, Kristin, (1989). *Sex Differences in Test Performance: A Survey of the Literature,* College Board Report No.89-3, College Entrance Examination Board, New York, N.Y.

Wily, Helen, (1986) Women in Mathematics. Some Gender Differences from the I.E.A. Survey in New Zealand. *New Zealand Mathematics Magazine,* Vol 23, No.2, pp29-49.

Willis, Sue, (1990) *'Real girls don't do maths': gender and the construction of privilege,* Deakin University Press, Deakin University, Victoria, Australia.

Young-Loveridge, Jenny, (1992). Department of Education Studies, University of Waikato. Background paper for the National Workshop on Professional Development in Educational Assessment, Educational Assessment Secretariat, Ministry of Education, Wellington, New Zealand.

Questions

- How could we raise the status of computational skills (compared with problem solving, for example)? Should we do this?
- Should we inform pupils which types of assessment are likely to be to their advantage? Which pupils should we inform? When?
- If you have to use a multiple choice test will it be fairer to pupils to penalise wrong answers or not? Why?
- Why may "records of authentic achievement" be preferable to a stand-alone examination result?
- Should mathematics examinations for the award of formal qualifications always have a gender balance of examiners?

Mathematics in Society

11 Innovation and the Mathematics Curriculum: Some Issues from the Past

Roger Openshaw

Discussion Questions

- Why do you think governments around the world assigned priority to the teaching of school mathematics and science during the 1960s?
- What factors influence curriculum innovation in mathematics at any given time?
- Is mathematics a male or a female dominated subject-discipline? Suggest some reasons why this might be so.
- Some writers have categorised school subject-disciplines as being of high status or low status. Where would you place school mathematics? What are the implications for mathematics curriculum innovation?

Innovation in New Mathematics: the Context

All innovation has a context and a place. Christchurch in the early 1960s was a small, unremarkable South Island city with its roots in nineteenth century Britain. In education, its apparently conservative exterior masked its importance as a mecca of learning. Here, far removed from the established centres of educational innovation in the Northern Hemisphere, one of the most significant changes to the school mathematics curriculum was about to take place. Gordon Knight, then a young secondary school mathematics teacher newly arrived from the United Kingdom, has recalled his surprise at discovering the city to be already the centre of experimentation in mathematics curricula. By this time, however, Christchurch possessed a longstanding tradition of curriculum reform which owed much to the

J. Neyland (ed), Mathematics Education: A Handbook for Teachers, Vol. 2, 110-121
© *1995 Wellington College of Education: New Zealand*

stimulus provided by the Christchurch Mathematics Group. That this tradition was to be continued was due in no small way to the determination of a particularly strong and energetic group of young city heads of department.

So far, so good. The difficulty is that even if one grants that Christchurch had an established tradition in mathematics innovation and more than its share of energetic teachers, we still need to account for the coming of the new mathematics to Christchurch at this particular juncture. Specifically, we need to explain the urgency which accompanied so much curriculum reform in this era, not just in mathematics, but in science, social studies and a number of other school subjects which also underwent veritable revolutions in content and in pedagogy at much the same time.

The first reason is a global one. The early '60s were an especially exciting time to be alive and young. The Space Race was in full swing and the USA and USSR were competing with each other in committing vast resources to the production of scientists and mathematicians. Western European nations were re-building their war-shattered economies and the new EEC was beginning to glimpse the glittering potential of economic union, sustained by the new technologies then everywhere evident. Even the normally conservative United Kingdom was pondering the merits of joining the Continent, while its industrialists and politicians eagerly sought to enlist the schools in boosting economic output in the interests of national prosperity.

In the United States, the United Kingdom and throughout Western Europe, this outburst of enthusiasm for mathematics and science was accompanied by an optimistic, even extravagant rhetoric from both politicians and the national press which set a premium on the efficient teaching of these subjects as national priorities. For their part, mathematicians and mathematics teachers were not slow to grasp the dazzling opportunities for what had been all too often, even in the relatively recent past, Cinderella subjects. While they too emphasised the role mathematics would place in the post-Sputnik era now dawning they also warned that, in order to fulfil its promise, school mathematics would have to be drastically changed. Old ways of thinking about the subject would have to go. 'New mathematics'(often emphatically termed 'Modern mathematics'), teaching would be firmly focused on understanding and concept-building rather than on narrow arithmetical calculation. Hand in glove with new ways of thought, would come a new pedagogy. Students, it was asserted, must be stimulated to proceed further in mathematics, rather than discouraged. Experimentation and an enlightened discussion of key theoretical concepts which had hitherto been reserved for the University or the research laboratory would supersede the rote-learning which still held pride of place in many classrooms.

At widely publicised conferences such as Royaumont, near Paris (late 1959), delegates from a variety of countries discussed the implications of the new developments for school mathematics. Such was the urgency that, by the middle of the '60s decade, well over one hundred curriculum projects aimed at introducing radical changes to future school mathematics programmes had been initiated. Of these the Yale-based School Mathematics Study Group (SMSG); the University of Illinois Committee on School Mathematics (UICS) and the British developed School Mathematics Project (SMP) were to be particularly influential in the New Zealand context.

So much for the Northern Hemisphere. In New Zealand too, there was excitement, but it was an excitement tempered to some extent by a general unease. The Empire which had given a degree of economic and strategic security was fast fading as Britain rapidly withdrew its forces from east of Suez. New Zealand's traditional place as the Mother-Country's out-lying farm was widely perceived to be in some jeopardy by the end of the 1950s. New Zealand governments in this era strove, less and less successfully, to balance diminishing export returns against a rising bill for imports. The national press, with its eyes on British negotiations with Europe, grimly and not altogether inaccurately forecast economic ruin if Britain eventually joined the European Economic Community (EEC).

Although in New Zealand, unlike Britain and the United States, there was no strong industrial sector to act as a catalyst, there was, nevertheless, pressure for change - any sort of change which might assist the country to transcend the twin tyranny of a dependent economy and geographical remoteness. Politicians talked vaguely of a future world dominated by maths, science, and technologically literate nations. Cabinet Ministers took up the new rhetoric and made it a feature of their annual Reports. In the heightened competition for funding that was a hallmark of the late '50s and early '60s, government departments were quick to follow suit. The Education Department took up the rhetoric of mathematical reform with particular enthusiasm. And, like their overseas counterparts, a growing number of New Zealand educators found a ready-made audience when they pointed to the vast and growing problems of teachers and pupils, as they strove to make sense of the existing mathematics syllabus.

They had a difficult and pressing task before them. Adequate when it had been introduced in the '40s, the secondary mathematics syllabus by the early '60s was facing a growing crisis of confidence as public and professional appreciation of the potentiality of mathematics for individual and nation soared way beyond existing constraints. Essentially, the old syllabus divided the school population into two streams. The first and largest stream were exposed to 'core mathematics', or what was more realistically termed by contemporaries; 'work-a-day arithmetic'. 'Work-a-day' arithmetic for many schools had come to be synonymous with the rote-learning of tables and arithmetical rules. Usually it also involved solving problems incorporating such useful themes as scone-making for girls and fencing quarter-acre sections for boys. By contrast the second and smallest stream was given a strong dose of so-called 'full mathematics'. Unlike core mathematics, full mathematics was intended for a small elite whose ultimate destination was the university and the learned professions. It was characterised by a somewhat dull, highly abstract formalism which, in the case of geometry, had changed little since Euclid's time. For many students, parents and even teachers, mathematics of any sort was often regarded with indifference, loathing or downright fear.

Given this state of affairs, it is evident that all the external catalysts for change were present in Christchurch, quite as much as they had been only a short time before in London, New York or Paris. External catalysts, however, although crucial, are only one side of the picture in any account of curriculum innovation. The other side of the picture concerns the agents of change - the innovators themselves. In Christchurch, a significant agency for change was to be a small group of young mathematics heads of department working within several city secondary schools. Originally, there were four in the group: David Goldsmith at Christchurch Boys' High School; Roy Strange at Burnside; Peter Parr at Aranui and Owen McDowell at Shirley Boys. As beginning teachers, these young men had met and studied together at the University of Canterbury. University mathematics at this time was itself undergoing revolutionary changes of its own. Exposed to the new mathematical theories brought into New Zealand by such scholars as John de la Bere, they were provoked into increasingly criticising the shortcomings of the existing school mathematics syllabus. If, for instance, such fascinating and fundamental notions as sets were an integral part of the new mathematics at university, then why could they not become a central part of school mathematics as well? The more questions they asked, the more inadequate the syllabus appeared and the more pressingly urgent, the need for change. For these young men, there could now be no turning back from the course they had set themselves upon.

At least initially, despite the rhetoric about the future role of mathematics and science, there was little tangible assistance from the Department of Education. Undaunted, the four followed in the footsteps of countless teachers who had preceded them. Some years before, a small group of social studies teachers had planned their own strategy for curriculum change in a crowded coffee bar in Auckland's Queen Street. It was all part and parcel of the Great Kiwi 'do-it-yourself' tradition in educational innovation. Now, once again, it was to be set in motion. Fortunately the Christchurch group realised fairly early that, whilst they had pressing responsibilities at their respective schools which militated against professional communication, they were also timetablers for their subjects and thus endowed with a degree of flexibility. It was enough. Through judicious re-allocation of class schedules they were able to allocate themselves one afternoon per week during which they were all simultaneously free to meet and to talk about mathematics.

They pooled their strengths and experiences, much as New Zealand teachers have done before and since. Goldsmith had personally observed SMSG in operation in the United States. Others in the group had obtained SMP material by writing to the project's British-based director, Dr Thwaites. An early influence on them all was Max Riske, then Deputy Principal of Wellington Technical College. Riske had spent five months in Illinois observing UICSM in late 1959 and had been particularly impressed with the emphasis this project placed on algebraic structure and discovery learning methods. From successive meetings and discussions came written schemes of work drawn from various sources. These, they tried out on specially selected classes in the four schools. Finally, the group produced their own textbook, the successive drafts of which had been laboriously typed out by the wives for trials in various local schools, with copies run off on a borrowed Gestetner. By this time the Department had recognised them sufficiently to grant them one working half day for curriculum development purposes.

In all of the above, I have stressed Christchurch. It should be emphasised, however, that these particular mathematics innovators were not to be alone for long. In Dunedin, Jack Herron was already thinking along similar lines. Neither were the innovators to be solely male. In Auckland, Margaret Laidlaw, a young Scottish migrant with an degree in mathematics from the University of Edinburgh (a rarity among rarities in early post-war New Zealand), was at that time a young teacher at Epsom Girls Grammar. To her way of thinking the existing mathematics syllabus did not encourage girls to question or to take an interest in mathematics. As acting head of department she resolved to institute fundamental changes within the school mathematics programme. This was no easy task. Along with the difficulties familiar to her male contemporaries as they strove to implement change Laidlaw, as the principal family breadwinner and care-giver, was obliged to do much of her work after 9.00pm, after the children had gone to bed. Nevertheless, at Epsom she set up a mathematics room complete with apparatus and insisted that all classes have a minimum of two periods a week in it. She produced a book for the third form and another for the fourth form, written up in her own handwriting. Reeds, the publishers, heard about it, somehow obtained a copy, and immediately offered her a contract. Incidentally, some of Laidlaw's original material is still in use in the 1990s; an indication, perhaps, of the quality of much of the early work.

Back in Christchurch, Helen Wily, a teacher at the independent girls' school, Rangi-ruru, was attending refresher courses on the new maths. She was inspired particularly by the enthusiasm of Max Riske, and, like Laidlaw, resolved to encourage girls to achieve in mathematics. She utilised the limited New Zealand material then available, along with an American text by Dolciani, Berman and Freilich called, *Modern Algebra: Structure and Method.* Dolciani, Wily would pointedly remind her students, was in fact *Mary* Dolciani - women too, could write mathematics texts. It was a salutary lesson for a generation of young women conditioned to believe that mathematics was men's work.

As the middle of the decade approached, local efforts conducted largely in isolation in various regional centres throughout New Zealand inexorably fused into a national movement for change. Refresher courses in the new mathematics became increasingly common. At a meeting in 1964 advocates were successful in lobbying the Department for additional funding for pilot programmes and for syllabus preparation. Politicians too, showed an interest in what had been done. In January 1965 Dr W.B. Sutch told a teachers refresher course in Wanganui that the Government and the country appreciated the recent efforts made in mathematics by enthusiastic and enlightened teachers - efforts which would lead to improvements in both economic and social life. A pilot School Certificate mathematics paper was introduced alongside the more traditional examination paper. Innovation was not just confined to secondary school mathematics. In primary and in intermediate schools too, plans were set in motion for new syllabuses quite unlike those which had preceded them. As the pace of reform increased, radio stations and women's magazines throughout the country ran features on the new maths for bewildered parents. By the end of the decade, school mathematics had, in syllabus and prescription terms, and to a lesser extent in classroom terms, been transformed. The new maths had arrived.

National enthusiasm for the new maths, however, was not to last.

By the mid 1970s, the oil shocks had underlined the country's economic vulnerability. All the scientists and mathematicians in the world, it seemed, could not fundamentally alter New Zealand's economic and geographical disadvantages. Simultaneously, cracks in both the conception and the process of innovation began to appear. Even during the heyday of the new mathematics, a number of well-placed critics had warned that the innovators had, by their assumption that mathematics could be taught more meaningfully by beginning with general and abstract principals, simply got their psychology wrong. Now, as optimism faded, they began to gather support. Overseas, in the United States, Britain and Western Europe, the pendulum began to swing back to less ambitious approaches. In New Zealand parents complained of a lack of basic skills such as they themselves had received as students. A new generation of senior pupils anxiously perused the dwindling columns of situations vacant in local newspapers. Employers grumbled that what they really wanted from school-leavers was simple counting skills and elementary calculations involving whole numbers, not an incomplete understanding of the structure of mathematics. An increasing number of politicians now threw their weight behind the new curriculum conservatism. For new mathematics as such, it was to be the end, though such a statement must immediately be qualified. Only in a few schools, did we ever really go back to the old mathematics. Certainly later syllabuses, developed in the '70s, gave some recognition to the change in attitude, and put more emphasis on the more mechanical aspects of the subject. It is equally true to say that, at least in some respects, the spirit that informed the original new maths innovations still remain to this day a feature of contemporary school mathematics at all educational levels.

Conclusion

What then, *should* we conclude about this particular curriculum innovation. Can we draw from it anything which might assist us in analysing educational change at other times, in other localities and even in other school subjects? I believe we can draw several conclusions. You might be able to add some others of your own.

The first and most obvious conclusion seems to be that all educational change has a social, political and economic context. This is particularly true of curriculum innovation in subjects which are widely perceived to have direct benefits to the national economy and to personal social mobility, such as mathematics. It might seem obvious, but one thing we should always be sure about is precisely *why* we are innovating, and what exactly it is that we are hoping to achieve. In virtually all countries where it was introduced, the new mathematics innovations were put into place amidst a time of widespread faith in the power of mathematics and science to have an immediate and beneficial impact upon the economic and social structure. Given the power of mathematics and science rhetoric to capture the imagination of politicians, big business, the press and the public, we should examine the effect of this peculiarly modern faith on curriculum reform in more detail.

In New Zealand during the early 1960s, growing interest in the power of mathematics to transform the fates of individuals and nations enabled innovators to put considerable and often successful pressure on the Education Department to provide resources. In part success (well, at least success in relation to other curriculum areas) came because, in the final analysis, the Department, having given lip-service to the central importance of mathematics in future national development was left a prisoner of its own rhetoric. Innovators were quick to remind the Department of its promises, even going so far as to publicly 'invite' the Department to discontinue any further support for 'modern approaches' to mathematics, precisely because they well knew that such a course was simply not viable in the context of the times.

To a large extent though, we may clear educators of charges that they cynically exploited contemporary prejudices. After all, given the traditional reluctance of politicians and bureaucrats to support any educational innovation where significant costs are incurred, educators can hardly be blamed for making the most of the comparatively rare times when national priorities and educational desirability are in step. Still, while we are on the subject, we might utilise our newly gained historical insight to examine recent attempts to introduce technology into the school curriculum, and, perhaps, the arguably rather vague claims being made on its behalf.

Second, this chapter suggests that, as innovators, we should always be aware of the ideological and theoretical underpinnings of major overseas educational projects. It was fortuitous for New Zealand innovators that as the new mathematics gained in popularity, the value of the major American projects were being enhanced by the apparent reconciliation of Brunerian structuralism with the theories of Piaget. Fortuitous because Piagetian principles had strongly influenced earlier changes to the Infant School Mathematics programme and any perceived conflict at this early stage may well have compromised efforts to implement changes across the entire educational sector. As it turned out, however, this reconciliation was more apparent than real. New Zealand secondary schools on the whole accepted the Brunerian notion of the spiral curriculum, and to a lesser extent the syllabuses intended for the upper primary schools and intermediate schools followed suit. Infant Departments retained their existing mathematics syllabus with its Piagetian framework, and this contributed to a major mismatch at the standard one level which was to plague mathematics teaching for many years to come. Furthermore, early secondary school innovators, as we have seen, were often eclectic in drawing upon overseas material. Successive school mathematics syllabuses for primary and then intermediate schools merely compounded the problem.

Third, my own research into the history of curriculum innovation in a number of subject-disciplines points to a need to ensure that we have a spread of expertise at all levels of the education system in the area where we are implementing changes. This is particularly relevant for mathematics, where those individuals who possess the appropriate combination of mathematical qualifications *and* educational qualifica- tions are still comparatively rare. Early new mathematics innovators possessed a virtual monopoly of expertise as publicists for the new approaches within what was, and remains still, a high-status subject-discipline. Moreover, the Education Department at the time had few staff with the mathematical background to comprehend the proposed changes and at least one contemporary observer has recalled with some amusement the sight of a disdainful Riske during an early new mathematics refresher course, striding up to the front of the room and pushing a newly appointed Departmental curriculum officer aside, to loudly condemn what he had said as totally fallacious nonsense. It would be difficult to contemplate such an incident occurring within the context of, say, social studies innovation over the same period.

When we turn to the actual mathematics classroom, it becomes transparently obvious that inadequate mathematical qualifications among a high proportion of contemporary teachers doomed the new programmes to relative failure in many schools. Although at the outset professional interest was undoubtedly considerable, and in-service courses were well attended, there were never enough of them and a high proportion of those who did attend possessed insufficient mathematical understanding to make the most of their opportunity. However, rather than look coldly and analytically at the whole problem of upgrading teacher skills, it was more convenient for officialdom to blame the programmes themselves - a strategy that became progress- ively more attractive as the economic situation declined during the 1970s. In primary schools these factors were, if anything, more evident than at the secondary level, even to the extent that an apparently informal remark from a highly placed Departmental source to the effect that the average pupil should cover two pages from the text per day, became progressively elevated to the status of an edict, enforced with frightening zealous efficiency by the professional educational hierarchy. In such an ethos, curriculum reform is rendered extremely problematic.

Then there are the pupils themselves to consider. The early innovators deliberately selected the top forms to experiment with. This practice was largely continued with the various pilot schemes. Such a phenomenon is not, of course, confined to new mathematics innovation during the 1960s, nor is it peculiar to mathematics as a curriculum subject. To the extent that untried concepts and teaching methods require development within a favourable environment, it might even be argued that is a defensible practice. Not withstanding this qualification though, we still need to ask serious questions about the aims of educational innovation and in particular, about the eventual outcome of specific curriculum changes once the 'average' teacher in the 'average' school working with 'average' and 'below average' students is involved in the process.

One should not finish, however, on a negative note. The new mathematics was a bold and courageous innovation which has had a significant impact on the way we think about school mathematics. It contributed in a major way to the development of a domestic school textbook industry. And without the dedication and energy of early new mathematics pioneers, we would probably still be asking boys to work out how much time it would take to mow the average section, and girls to work out problems involving the bottling of immense quantities of homemade jam. If we are still not entirely convinced, then perhaps we should end our story with that same British high school teacher, now a respected university Professor of Mathematics who, as a young new-arrival in Christchurch was so impressed with the early stages of new mathematics innovation. His verdict? "To some extent, you have to live with it." "I mean, the alternative is not to innovate... and so avoid the problem." Such is the perennial dilemma of the curriculum innovator.

Further Reading

Much of this chapter is based on two principal sources:
(a) the testimony contained in a series of interviews with mathematics teachers who were involved in new mathematics curriculum reform during the 1960s. Transcripts of this testimony appear in; R. Openshaw (1991), *Schooling in the 40s and 50s: An Oral History*, Research Resources No.1. It is published by the Educational Research and Development Centre, Massey University, Palmerston

North, and is readily obtainable from them.

(b) a recent paper completed by the author which analyses in some detail the process of reform in mathematics, using the new maths as a case study. See, R. Openshaw, "New Zealand Secondary Schools and the coming of the new mathematics", *SAME Papers*, 1992, pp.140-157.

Further Discussion

- Reconsider the first discussion question again in the light of what you have read. Why does innovation in school mathematics, (or for that matter, any educational change), take place? Which factors are, relatively speaking, the most important? International, national or local?
- Under what circumstances might mathematics curriculum innovation be successful?
- How significant do you think the efforts of female teachers were in the 1960s in raising the consciousness of today's generation of young women with regards to mathematics?
- What features might doom mathematics curriculum innovation to likely failure? What, exactly, constitutes failure, in this context?
- If in the long-term all educational innovation loses a little of its original impetus, should we even bother to try at all?
- What lessons (if any), can contemporary mathematics curriculum innovators learn from history?

(Selected) Bibliography

Appendices to the Journals of the House of Representatives, 1958-1966.

Bull, M.A. (1960). *The qualifications and supply of mathematics teachers*, Studies in Education No.18. Wellington: NZCER.

Clark, A.E.E. (1960). *Mathematics in post-primary schools*, Auckland: MA dissertation.

Clark, M.J. (1977). *An investigation into the New Zealand Forms 1-4 mathematics syllabus*, Victoria: MA dissertation.

Cooper, B. (1985). *Renegotiating secondary school mathematics. A study of curriculum change and stability*, Studies in Curriculum History No.3. London: Falmer.

Khan, G.I.A.R. (1990). The politics of curriculum innovation in Lauder, H. & Wylie, C. *Towards successful schooling*. Hampshire:

Falmer Press, 121-137.

McCausland, J. (1974). Innovation in new mathematics courses. *New Zealand Mathematics Magazine,* 11, 1 (April 1974): 32-36.

Massey, L.E. (1980). *An analysis of curriculum change: Official statement and actual practice: An attempt at an historical and sociological reconstruction of curriculum change in New Zealand secondary schools with particular reference to the teaching of science and English since the Thomas Report,* Auckland: D.Phil. dissertation

Moon, B. (1986). *The "new maths" curriculum controversy. An international story.* London: Falmer Press.

Murdoch, J.H. (1950). *The Teaching of Mathematics in Post Primary Schools.* Wellington: NZCER.

New Zealand Department of Education (1943). *The post-primary school curriculum. Report of the committee appointed by the Minister of Education in November 1942 (the Thomas Report).* Wellington: Government Printer.

New Zealand Parliamentary Debates 1958-1966.

Openshaw, R. (1992). Subject Construction and Reconstruction: Social Studies and the New Mathematics, in McCullough, Gary (ed.) *The School Curriculum in New Zealand: History, Theory, Policy and Practice.* Palmerston North: Dunmore Press, pp201-218.

Riske, M. (1961). Re-thinking our mathematics. *PPTA Journal,* 8, 10 (November): 20-22.

Scott, R.A. (1962-63). *Teacher Training including some references to new developments in the teaching of science and mathematics. A New Zealand assessment.* Report presented to the University of London.

Struthers, J. (1964). Experimental work in mathematics in New Zealand schools. *New Zealand Mathematics Magazine,* 5, 1: 2-7.

Werry, B.W. (1980). *Mathematics in New Zealand secondary schools.* Wellington: NZCER.

12 Calculating a Square Root Before the Electronic Age

Stan Roberts

Introduction

I am going to outline five methods of finding the square root. These methods involve using pencil and paper, or machines worked either by hand or by electricity.

In previous times, most calculations were performed using pencil and paper (helped by a rubber to erase the multiplicity of errors), and a book of tables if one was fortunate enough to possess one. All the calculations depended, as is still the case today, on the four fundamentals of arithmetic: addition, subtraction, multiplication, and division, with the latter three depending on the first.

Subtraction: If we wish to subtract 7 from 10, we ask 'What number needs to be *added* to get 10?'

Multiplication: If we *add* three 4s together we get 12, so we write 3 x 4 = 12, and thus build up our multiplication table.

Division: Division is simply multiplication, since for example, to divide 35 by 8 we ask 'What is the greatest *multiple* of 8 which is less than 35?'

Long Division: This is an extension of division when the divisor has more than one digit. We use the algorithm illustrated by the following example. To calculate the division 59644 ÷ 37 the method of solution is:

```
        1612
   37)59644
      37↓↓↓
      226↓↓
      222↓↓
        44↓
        37↓
        74
        74
```

Since 37 will divide into 59 only once, a 1 is written above the 9, and 37 is subtracted from the 59, giving the number 22; the 6 is brought down next to the 22, and we then find that 37 divides into 226 six times. With some practice this problem would take a bright child about a minute to solve. While we were able to do the mechanical computations required, none of us ever knew why it worked, nor, I would think, did any of the teachers. Just as today, when only the specialist knows how the calculator achieves its results. Some of the methods below depend on the ability of a person to *accurately* use long division.

The First Method: Newton's Method
The first method I will outline for finding the square root is Newton's Method, presumably invented by Sir Issac Newton (1642 - 1727). There obviously must have been earlier methods, since Pythagoras made calculations concerning the length of a diagonal of a square with sides of unit length (and was disturbed when he found that it was impossible to compute this exactly). To trace all methods used in the past would need a study of mathematical history.

Consider the following three divisions:

```
              4 (quotient)          5           6
   (divisor) 4)16                  5)25         6)36
```

We can see that in each case the divisor is the same as the quotient. When this happens, the divisor, or the quotient, is called the square root of the number. The number being divided is called a perfect square in such a case. But suppose we want to find the square root of a number which is not a perfect square, such as 32. We use a process called *iteration*, which is another name for *trial and error*. In this case we first guess a number to be used as the divisor, which we think about right, and the better the guess, the faster we get the answer. From the above examples, it can be seen that the square root must lie between 5 and 6, so let us choose an average of 5 and 6, that is, 5.5, found by adding 5 + 6 and dividing the answer by 2. We make our first iteration by using long division

$$
\begin{array}{r}
5.8 \\
5.5\overline{)32.000} \\
\underline{27.5} \\
4.50 \\
\underline{4.40}
\end{array}
$$

Since the divisor and quotient are *different*, we know that the square root is between these two values. So we make our second iteration using the average, of 5.5 and 5.8, that is, 5.65, and we find the quotient to be 5.66. For our third iteration we use 5.655 for the divisor, and then keep going for as long as we wish. Such a method is very long-winded using pencil and paper, but is ideal for programming into a computer. It is also very good for a *mathematical* exercise, since we can easily see how the result is obtained. This method would also be useful in an examination if the square root button on the calculator failed. It was a brilliant idea of Newton's.

The Second Method
The second method is similar to the former but uses multiplication instead of division. Suppose we want to find the square root of 70, say.

Iteration 1: Guess a number and square it. Perhaps take 8, which has a square of 64, so a larger number is required.

Iteration 2: 9 with a square of 81 is too large, so take an average (8.5).

Iteration 3: 8.5 has a square of 72.25; take the average of 8 and 8.5.

Iteration 4: 8.25 has a square of 68.06. And so on.

The Third Method

This method has the advantage of speed, when using pencil and paper, but has the disadvantage that no one (apart from a specialist) can possibly understand why it works. But it *does* work, and it *is* fast. It was taught in the secondary schools for many years, certainly in the 1920s and 30s. It was taught in the fifth form, at the end of which one sat the Matriculation (UE) exam, and almost invariably a problem was set in the exam such as: Find the square root of 51679.4321, correct to two decimal places.

```
                              5'16'79.43'21
          2                   4 ↓↓ ↓↓↓↓↓↓
          2                   116
         42                   84 ↓↓
          2                   32 79
        447                   31 29 ↓↓
          7                   1 50 43
       4543                   1 36 29 ↓↓
          3                   14 14 21
      45463                   13 63 89
          3                   50 32
      45466
```

So square root = 227.33

Step 1: Starting from the decimal position and working outwards, place a comma behind or in front of each second digit. In this example we see that there would thus be, in the square root, three digits to the left of the decimal position.

Step 2: 'What is the square root of the greatest perfect square less than 5?' The greatest perfect square less than 5 is 4, and its square root is 2. So we write 2, starting a new column well over to the left of our given number, and then write 4 under the 5.

Step 3: Under the 2 on the left, add another 2, and get 4. On the right subtract the 4 from the 5 and get 1, and then bring down the next two digits 1 and 6, and line them up with the 1, obtaining the number 116.

Step 4: We now must think of the 4 on the left as being 40. We ask 'What is the greatest number between 40 and 49 (inclusive), which, when multiplied by its second digit, is less than 116?' For example, 43 x 3 = 129, but this is greater than 116, so we try 42 x 2 which = 84, which is less than 116.

Step 5: The 4 on the left becomes 42, and we add another 2 to it, and it becomes 44. We subtract 84 from the 116 and get 32. Then bring down the next 2 digits 79, giving the number 3279.

Step 6: 'What is the greatest number between 440 and 449 (inclusive), which, when multiplied by the third digit, is less than 3279. It turns out to be 447: 447 x 7 = 3129.

Step n: Keep going until enough digits are found to give the specified accuracy.

Answer: This is found by taking the final digit of each iteration. This particular example took me 90 seconds to calculate. (Newton's method took me 8 minutes using 4 iterations, with far greater possibilities of error, since the large original number must be written down for each iteration.) This secondary school method was taught to us when I was at an educational course in the Air Force in 1944.

The fourth method
The fourth method was used by the Applied Mathematics Division of the DSIR, for 20 years (1945 - 1965), using a Monro-Matic electric calculator. This machine was about the same size and weight as an old Remington Typewriter. It was packed absolutely full of moving mechanical parts. It had a keyboard of 10 x 10 numbers, with two registers. For additions or subtractions the upper register gave the number of operations used in the computation, and the lower register gave the sum. The method used was based on the mathematical theorem 'The sum of the first n odd integers is equal to n^2 '. This is set out in the following table:

Integers	Odd Integers	Sum of Successive Odd Integers
1	1	1
2	3	4
3	5	9
4	7	16
5	9	25
6	11	36

We can see that the sum of the first 6 odd integers is 36 i.e., 6^2. If this process is reversed, we subtract the odd integers successively. If we subtract from 36 the numbers 1, 3, 5, 7, 9, 11 successively, we get 35, 32, 27, 20, 11, 0. To arrive at 0, we needed 6 subtractions, so the square root of 36 is therefore 6.

With the Monro-Matic, we first entered the 36 into the lower register, and subtracted the odd numbers as above, and the upper register told us that there had been 6 operations, which was the square root of the number entered. This same method can be used with numbers which are not perfect squares (see DSIR Applied Mathematics, Publications and Personal Recollections, published in September 1993). It is an extremely fast method, and from memory, the square root of an eight digit number could be found with eight significant digits in something less than 20 seconds.

The Fifth Method
The fifth method is to use a book of tables. In 1814 Peter Barlow of the Royal Military Academy at Woolwich, England, produced a magnificent book of tables for all integers up to 12,500, with functions such as Square, Cube, Square Root, Cube Root, etc. It has up to 80,000 entries, some of them containing as many as 14 digits. I have no idea how the calculations were made, but it must have been an horrendous task. In his preface Peter Barlow says 'The only motive which prompted me in this unprofitable task was the utility that I conceived might result from my labour.' They have in fact been exceptionally useful for many mathematical computations for well over 150 years.

Now that the electronic calculator is here to stay, we have no need to use any of the above five methods. Unfortunately, the square root button on the calculator is simply a piece of magic which gives the right answer. While this is a very useful tool for computing, it gives no *understanding* as to how one is able to derive a square root. I think the best method from a *mathematical* point of view, is that of Newton, which today would be part of 'Numerical Methods'. It would not take much effort to calculate the square root of an integer less than, say, 100 correct to one decimal place, by this method.

13　Why Some Mathematics Texts Seem Obscure

Lindsay Johnston

Introduction

If you asked a group of working mathematicians and mathematics teachers what the essence of mathematics is, you would get some quite different answers such as 'logical reasoning in a mathematical context' or 'an intuitive grasp of the shape of mathematical structures'. This is not because some answers would be wrong but because the activities of mathematics are extremely varied; different areas involve quite different activities. There are, however, some themes which are common to the development of most mathematics; two of these, which are the subject of this paper, are the themes of increasing *formality* and increasing *generality*. I will begin by giving examples of these aspects of mathematical development before discussing their relevance to mathematics teaching and learning and then giving further examples. The emphasis of the paper is on teaching mathematics as a subject area although much reference will be made to mathematical activities. Frequent reference will be made to *problem solving* activities which I take to be activities aimed at finding an answer to a question or investigating a situation where the path to the outcome or answer is not immediately obvious. Clearly, what is a problem solving activity for one pupil may not be for another; it depends upon ability, prior knowledge, and prior experience.

Formality

Formality in mathematics can be thought of as the manipulation of symbols without regard to their meaning. I am extending this idea to the solving of mathematical "problems" by automatic processes which require little or no thought and to the idea that the less thinking that is required for a mathematical process, the more formal it is. At first

J. Neyland (ed), Mathematics Education: A Handbook for Teachers, Vol.2, 129-136
© *1995 Wellington College of Education: New Zealand*

sight this may appear to be quite foreign to our notions of the ideal of mathematics which almost certainly put 'understanding' and 'thinking' as an essential part of mathematical activity. Formal activity is only a part of mathematics but it must be recognised as a legitimate part if mathematics is to be seen as a whole. It is ironic that in many situations the whole aim of mathematical development is towards an end point where questions, which started out as genuine problems, can be answered without thought. This applies not only to the historical development of mathematics but also to its development in our minds as we learn it. For example, consider the problem of discovering whether or not a quadratic equation has distinct real roots. There are a number of related pieces of mathematics such as:

(1) Discovering that a quadratic equation can have at most two real roots;
(2) Discovering that the graph of a quadratic function is always a parabola;
(3) Finding a technique for solving a quadratic equation and discovering whether or not it has a real solution (completing the square, for instance).

The mathematics involved in the above can be a rich source of activity and problems, all of which may be directed towards answering the original question of whether or not a particular quadratic equation has two distinct real roots.

Whether or not the question posed here was a central one historically it can be seen that out of a great deal of mathematical activity, which would have involved (i), (ii) and (iii), has come the idea of the *discriminant* of a quadratic which enables anyone who can interpret a formula and do basic arithmetic to answer the question as to whether or not a given quadratic equation has distinct real roots. No real thought and certainly no problem solving is required to answer the question; in fact it can be answered by a computer and that is the ultimate check that no thought is required. Thus, what started out as a relatively difficult mathematical problem becomes a question which can be answered by an automatic process. This is not an isolated case; much of the development of mathematics can be interpreted as finding ways of converting difficult problems into questions which can be answered algorithmically by people who would have had no chance of solving the original problems. Nor is the increase in formality confined to problem solving situations; as we learn the basic arithmetic addition facts we are likely to have learned how to discover the value of $7 + 8$ by some process like counting on fingers. Whether or not we consciously learned tables of facts by rote we now recall the value of $7 + 8$ from memory without thought. This lack of necessary thought obviously makes using the simple facts of addition much more efficient and so it is with many of the situations where mathematics becomes more formal as it develops. More examples will be discussed later.

Most algebraic manipulation is a formal activity. If we need to reflect on the reasons why each step is true then progress is painfully slow and what we can do with mathematics becomes severely limited. There are numerous examples which illustrate the fact that for efficient learning we must accept that some facts and processes must be learned so that they can be used almost without thought.

Generality

One concept or method in mathematics is more general than another if the second is a special case of the first. Consider the following two problems:

(i) \$100 is deposited in a bank account at the beginning of each month and interest is compounded at a rate of 0.5% per month. How much money is in the account at the end of 12 months? Provided the formula for compound interest in known, the required amount can be written down as $100 (1.005)^{12} + 100 (1.005)^{11} + 100(1.005)^{10} + ... + 100 (1.005)^2 + 100 (1.005)$. The arithmetic operations can then be carried out and the final value of the investment is thus found.

(ii) Find the value of the repeating decimal $0.1515...$. One way of approaching the problem is to write down the number x as

$$x = \frac{15}{10^2} + \frac{15}{10^4} + \frac{15}{10^6} + \ldots$$

Hence $$10^2 x = 15 + \frac{15}{10^2} + \frac{15}{10^4} + \frac{15}{10^6} + \ldots = 15 + x$$

Hence $$99 x = 15 \quad \text{and} \quad x = \frac{15}{99}.$$

Clearly both problems give rise to *geometric series*, one a finite series and the other, infinite. That is, the original problems can be solved as applications of the more general idea of geometric series. In the same way, a geometric series can be seen as a special kind of series and some of its properties may be discovered by knowing results which hold for *any* series.

This too, is not an isolated example. As mathematics develops it is frequently the case that the concepts and methods of the previous decade or century are special cases of those of the present and as we learn mathematics the concepts we learn today are likely to be special cases of those we learn in the future.

Formality and Generality in Mathematics Education

The increasing formality and generality of mathematics as it develops are very relevant to mathematics teachers for several reasons. These will be discussed in what follows.

Formality: It is a very common point of view among modern mathematics educators that problem solving activities and discovery learning methods should be emphasised in the classroom. There is a very good reason for this; the skills learned through problem solving and discovery learning are *general skills* and may be expected to transfer and have application in other, possibly non-mathematical, aspects of a child's life. Many children will never need to apply some of the specific mathematical methods they learn about but we have faith that the general skills they learn will be of benefit to them in other areas of their lives. It should be realised, however, that problem solving activities are not the whole of mathematics. Mathematicians have, over the centuries, built up a huge body of knowledge, much of which is relevant today. We cut our pupils off from this knowledge, and from the richer source of problem solving material which it makes available, if we ignore formal methods which must be learned if pupils are to efficiently become familiar with significant areas of mathematics. A mathematics teacher is involved in two types of teaching which, of course, overlap to some extent. The first is the teaching of general skills; some such skills which are mentioned in the new curriculum document are "applying mathematical ideas and techniques to unfamiliar problems in everyday life", "the ability to carry out logical and systematic thinking", "the ability to see patterns and relationships", and "the ability to think abstractly". The other is the teaching of the subject matter of mathematics. Both are important but apart from everyday mathematics, the latter has particular importance only for pupils who are likely to apply mathematics in other subject areas or who are likely to want to study mathematics for its own sake. Nevertheless, all pupils can benefit from a knowledge of the content of mathematics; it is a rich source of problems which can lead to the pupils learning more complex skills.

I have argued that formal methods are necessary to teach the content of mathematics efficiently; this is necessary so that pupils will learn the mathematics they need in everyday life but also because mathematics is an important body of knowledge within which pupils can learn general problem solving skills.

Suppose, in population studies, we are interested to know how long it will take a population to double if it is increasing by 5% per year. After some problem solving activities, which I believe would help a pupil to learn some general skills, the problem may be reduced to the equation

$$P \ (1.05)^n \ = \ 2P.$$

The solving of this equation could be regarded as a further problem and a pupil may well acquire general skills by attempting to solve it. But if the formal methods for solution of such equations are known then the original problem is effectively solved as soon as the equation is written down. The knowledge of the formal method shortens the solution of the original problem leaving the pupil with time to attempt a wider variety of and a larger number of problems. It is also the case that this equation would never be solved by many pupils if it was left as a problem for them; if the methods of solving such equations are taught by the methods of traditional text books then problems which have much more intrinsic interest can be used for pupils to develop their problem solving skills. *The knowledge of formal methods is one of the aspects of mathematics which allows us to build on the work of previous generations of mathematicians without repeating all of their discoveries.* What pupils do in the classroom must be a mixture of activities which should include learning to use some methods and facts without the need to think about them. There may even be a good case for learning some facts by rote.

Generality: Consider the problem of finding the slope of a graph at a given point. In a typical course students will first be shown or be guided into discovering how to find the slope of

$$y \ = \ x^2 \qquad \text{at } x \ = \ 3.$$

A next step may then be to find the derived function of $y = x^2$; i.e., to find the slope at a variable point, x, of the domain. A further step may then be to find derived function of x^n for $n \in N$. A fourth step may be to find the derived function of any polynomial.

In this process what is discovered at each step is a special case of what follows; that is, each step is a generalisation of the previous one.

The general point of view provided by knowing how to find the derivative of any polynomial clearly has much wider application than the knowledge of how to find the slope of the graph of a particular power of x at a particular point.

The generalising process is a natural development in many mathematical areas; concepts are generalised as are methods and strategies. The student who grasps the general point of view has a wider range of applications available and if students are able to grasp a general concept or method from examples of special cases then they may be able to apply the concept or method to quite different examples from those in relation to which it was learned. This is the process of *transfer of learning* which must be the aim of all our teaching; mathematics is the ideal subject area in which to practise it. The process of generalisation is central to all education. It is important in mathematics education, where the process is very explicit, to ensure that students are aware of the process as well as learning concepts and methods in the most general form they can.

It is popularly believed that concepts are best grasped by seeing examples of that concept; for example one may introduce the idea of the angle standing on an arc of a circle by showing diagrams of some particular circles and lines. Most teachers would regard this as preferable to writing down a general description as a first step. However, it is also important that pupils *ultimately* grasp concepts in the most general way they can; they will then be able to see more special cases of the concept and in the example mentioned, they will be more likely to be able to pick out two angles on the same arc from a complex diagram. In some cases this may involve learning a general definition, or as in this case, it may involve learning a general process which will enable one to find all the angles on a given arc. Thus, it is usually not the best plan to introduce concepts or methods in a general way but it is important to lead pupils towards a general understanding.

Formality and Generality in Context

An oversimplified summary of the above ideas is as follows. In the process of developing mathematics, mathematicians are involved in a variety of problem solving activities such as those listed from the new curriculum document. It is these sorts of activity which we see as developing general skills in our pupils and, therefore, being desirable for all pupils. The end point of the development of mathematics is a formal and general structure and mathematics is often presented in text books in this form. While it is essential that we involve our pupils in problem solving activities it is also desirable that they learn some formal methods and some general concepts; formal methods enable them to learn content more efficiently, and general concepts have wider applicability as well as encouraging transfer of learning. Learning the content of mathematics is important because it is applicable in every-day situations as well as in other subject areas. It is also important because it provides an ideal context in which to practise problem solving skills.

Difficulties with teaching in a formal or general way

I have stated that as an area of mathematics develops it tends to become more formal and more general in its application. The same is true of our *understanding* of an area of mathematics. What is presented in most text books is the result of these two development processes; the development of the subject matter historically and the development of the author's understanding. Unfortunately, as many of us know too well, what is crystal clear to the author can be quite obscure to the reader. This is not necessarily because the reader is lacking knowledge of some prerequisite facts, it is likely to be because the text book presentation is too formal or too general.

Supposing that the concept of standard deviation of a set of data is to be taught. A text book may begin by writing down

The standard deviation of $x_1, x_2 \ldots x_n$ is $\sigma = \sqrt{\dfrac{\sum\limits_{i=1}^{n} (x_i - \bar{x})^2}{n-1}}$

where $\bar{x} = \dfrac{\sum x_i}{n}$.

This is a very efficient statement, both general and formal, but it is very unlikely to have any meaning at all to 6th form pupils just being introduced to statistics even though they may in some sense know what all the symbols mean. On the other hand, to the book's author and to a mathematician who is very familiar with the symbolism it may be very meaningful and be an efficient way of becoming familiar with the concept. The formula above is general in that it applies to any finite set of data and it is formal in that for most pupils the symbols would have much less immediate meaning than some equivalent statement in everyday language. This lack of immediate meaning in the symbolism is clearly dependent on who is reading the formula; it is not until the symbols are part of a completely familiar language that a reader will find the formula clear and meaningful. It is a matter of common experience to all teachers that if concepts or methods are introduced to pupils in a way which is too general or too formal then pupils will have extreme difficulty and will not learn. On the other hand, as they become more experienced they are able to cope with more formality and more generality and take advantage of this experience to learn more efficiently. For example some pupils would see immediately that $\sum (x_i - \bar{x})^2$ is positive but others would not and would need at least to see special cases before they knew why that was so.   Different pupils learn most efficiently in different ways; what teachers must beware of is assuming that what is the most efficient final form of an area of mathematics in their minds or in the text book is the form in which pupils will most easily learn it. Teachers need to find the best balance for their pupils between being too general or formal and having pupils understand nothing and, at the other extreme, concentrating exclusively on particular examples which may be easily understood but lead to inefficient learning.

Social Issues

14   Beliefs and Values in Mathematics Education: An Outline of Ernest's Model

Jim Neyland

Discussion

Take each of the following sentence-pairs in turn and decide which sentence (A or B) is closest to your point of view.

A:	All learning involves periods of uncertainty, confusion and questioning.
B:	Mathematics should be presented in a sequence of simple steps so as to avoid confusion.

A:	The curriculum should be determined by experts and student opinion is of little value.
B:	Students should have a significant role in negotiating their curriculum.

A:	Mathematics is taught primarily to give students skills to use in employment.
B:	Mathematics is taught primarily to encourage in students a critical awareness of the world and society.

Introduction

When you made your choices from the above sentence pairs, you were drawing on your beliefs and values about teaching, learning, the teacher's role, the learner's role, the nature of mathematics, and so on. Some of your beliefs and values will be explicit and easily described,

J. Neyland (ed), Mathematics Education: A Handbook for Teachers, Vol.2, 139-149
© 1995 Wellington College of Education: New Zealand

others will be tacit and harder to identify. In this chapter I am going to outline how one mathematics educator, Paul Ernest, went about describing, and in some ways explaining, the range of beliefs held about mathematics teaching[1], and how these views can be linked with specific groups within society. Ernest published his analysis in a book called *The Philosophy of Mathematics Education*. I cannot do justice to this book in the few pages which make up this chapter, but I shall try to give you a feel for the approach Ernest adopts.

Ernest designed a framework of personal (subjective) belief systems. He based this framework, or model, on (i) the Perry theory, (ii) the distinction between absolutist and fallibilist notions of mathematics, (iii) Gilligan's distinction between separated and connected judgements, and (iv) an analysis of the beliefs of certain groups within society. The model enables us to look critically at curriculum statements, teaching resources, teaching approaches, and so on, and form answers to questions such as: *Whose* aims for mathematics teaching are expressed here? And *whose* view of mathematics is being promoted here?

The Perry Theory

The Perry theory (Perry, 1970) is an outline of some of the different ways people make intellectual and moral judgments. In brief, the Perry theory is based on the assumption that a person's intellectual and ethical development begins with an unquestioned set of beliefs, moves through several positions of detachment from these beliefs, and finally assumes a position of commitment to a set of intellectual and ethical principles. The following four statements reflect three different forms of moral reasoning.

* I was taught from the cradle that stealing is wrong under all circumstances.
* Some people think stealing is OK, some don't. People have to make their own judgements. I can't judge their actions.
* Sometimes stealing is defensible; sometimes not. The way to decide is to apply certain universal moral principles, such as: the right to life must

---

[1]A number of others have written on the topic of beliefs and values in education and mathematics education; see for example, Skilbeck (1976), Lawton (1983), Bishop (1988), Ellerton and Clements (1994), Neyland (1995a and 1995b), Boston, Haig and Lauder (1988), Belenky et al. (1986), and Barton in this volume.

take precedence over the right to property.

- The morality of stealing depends entirely on the particular circumstances. In order to make a judgement I would first need to understand the personal situations of everyone involved. Why do they feel they need to steal? Are they responsible for the care of children? and so on.

Ernest selects *Dualism, Multiplicity* and *Relativism* as representative of Perry's positions.

Dualism

The Dualist views the world in polarities of right/wrong, black/white, we/they, good/bad. They are passive, dependent on authorities to define truth and to teach right from wrong. The Dualist gradually becomes aware of a diversity of opinion and shifts to the Multiplistic position.

Multiplicity

Here it is recognised that authorities may not have all the right answers in some areas. There are many different points of view, but there is no basis for rational choice between them. "Everyone has a right to his or her own opinion, and mine is as good as any other." By starting to seek evidence and support for their opinion they gradually shift to the Relativist position.

Relativism

Here an evaluative approach to knowledge and values is consciously cultivated. A plurality of points of view, interpretations, frames of reference and value systems is recognised. Knowledge and choices are seen as dependent upon the particular context and are evaluated or justified within principled or rule governed systems.

It is important to note that the Perry theory is not about the *content* of a person's attitudes and judgements. It is about the *forms* of knowing, seeing and caring which a person uses.

Discussion

Discuss the following statements about mathematics teaching in the light of Perry's positions.

- There is only one way to teach maths. It is the way I was taught. I cannot conceive of any other approach.
- There are lots of ways of teaching maths, all equally valid. Personally, I'm not very good at maths so I integrate it with my social studies and art programmes.

- There are lots of ways of teaching maths, all equally valid. Personally, I'm not very good at maths so I use this mastery learning resource. The students do two worksheets a day.
- There are lots of ways of teaching maths, all equally valid. Personally, I did a maths degree specialising in pure maths, so I use a similar pure, axiomatic approach when teaching.
- There are lots of ways of presenting maths in the classroom. Each has strengths and weaknesses. I try and choose the approach most suitable for the class in question and most applicable to the focus of the lesson, and with a view to achieving a balance over the year.

Personal Beliefs about Mathematics

The Perry theory can be used to outline different ways of thinking about mathematics. These *personal* beliefs are not the same as the *public* philosophies of mathematics, which are explicitly stated and subject to critical analysis. Personal beliefs about mathematics are more private and some are tacit; and they influence how we teach. If you believe mathematics to be a highly organised body of knowledge, out there in a special mathematical world of abstract symbols and concepts, you will probably teach mathematics in a different way from the person who believes that mathematics is what mathematicians do, and that mathematical knowledge is just the socially agreed product of this activity.

Dualistic views of mathematics regard it as concerned with facts, rules, correct procedures and simple truths determined by absolute authority. Mathematics is viewed as fixed and exact; it has a unique structure. Doing mathematics is following the rules.

In Multiplistic views of mathematics multiple answers and multiple routes to an answer are acknowledged, but regarded as equally valid, or a matter of personal preference. Not all mathematical truths, the paths to them or their applications are known, so it is possible to be creative in mathematics and its applications. However, criteria for choosing from this multiplicity are lacking.

Relativistic views of mathematics acknowledge multiple answers and approaches to mathematical problems, and that their evaluation depends on the mathematical system, or its overall context. Likewise mathematical knowledge is understood to depend on the system or frame adopted, and especially on the inner logic of mathematics, which provide principles and criteria for evaluation.

(Ernest, 1991)

The Multiplistic position is illustrated by children who see mathematics as a mass of rules from which they make random selections in an effort to achieve the required answer. They view mathematics as a 'wild goose chase' in which they are chasing particular answers . . . not a rational and logical subject in which [one] can verify . . . answers by an independent process.

(Erlwanger, 1973)

Similarly, this position is illustrated by people who use statistical formulae and models uncritically, choosing a particular tool from a range of alternatives on the grounds of personal preference or expediency. Thus it is acknowledged that there are a multiplicity of answers and methods but there is no reasoned basis for choice.

Discussion
Illustrate the Dualist and Relativist positions for mathematical thinking.

Absolutism and Fallibilism

We have discussed a range of *personal* perspectives on mathematics. But there are *publicly debated* philosophies of mathematics, too. Ernest classifies the public philosophies into two categories, Absolutism and Fallibilism.

Absolutism
This viewpoint holds that mathematics contains certain and unchallengeable truths; that it is a body of certain knowledge. Axioms, definitions, and rules of inference are used to provide a precise description of the development of, and justification for, mathematical truth.

Fallibilism
This viewpoint sees mathematical truth as fallible. Mathematical concepts and proofs can never be regarded as beyond revision and correction; they may require renegotiation as standards of rigour change or new meanings emerge. Mathematics is what mathematicians do with all the imperfections inherent in any human activity or creation. Mathematics is a dialogue between people exploring mathematical problems, and it must be viewed in its historical and social context.

Both of these philosophical positions are Relativistic. Take a moment and convince yourself why.

However, there are private counterparts to these public philosophies, and these are not necessarily Relativistic. Ernest complements the Perry theory, which you will recall is about *forms* of moral and intellectual development, with a *content* which identifies personal views about the nature of mathematics. He argues that Absolutism has private counterparts in each of the three Perry positions. The Dualist/Absolutist position has an emphasis on mathematics as true facts and correct procedures, validated by an authority. Mathematical ideas are either absolutely true, or false. The Multiplistic/Absolutist position views mathematics as an unquestioned set of facts and procedures but with no particular set of principles, or authoritative source, to determine between them. The Relativist/Absolutist position views mathematical knowledge as certain and that there are rational grounds for justifying this.

A further personal position, Relativist/Fallibilist, is also possible. Here mathematics is viewed as never beyond correction, but that accepted mathematical knowledge can be justified and evaluated within particular frameworks of reason and social analysis.

Separated and Connected Positions

Ernest complements the Perry theory further by drawing on the categories of Separated and Connected judgements outlined by Gilligan (1982). He broadens these ways of *judging* to include notions of separated and connected ways of *knowing*, and then combines them with Perry's Relativist position with which they are consistent.

The Separated Position
This view has a focus on rights, abstract laws, universal principles, blind justice, objectivity and impartiality. Moral problems are seen as involving competing rights, and are resolved by formal, structured, and abstract reasoning, stripped of contextual factors.

The Connected Position
Here the focus is on relationships, care, and understanding the context and the human dimensions of a situation. Moral problems are seen as involving conflicting responsibilities and are resolved by contextual forms of thinking and dialogue leading to a creative consensus. The Connected thinker is willing to make exceptions to rules, look for weaknesses in particular solutions and identify remaining conflicts.

Positions on Mathematics Education

Ernest combined the positions outlined above to form the following five positions: *Dualist/Absolutist, Multiplistic/Absolutist, Relativist/Absolutist/Separated, Relativist/Absolutist/Connected,* and *Relativist/Fallibilist.* Why didn't he divide Relativist/Fallibilism into Separated and Connected divisions as he did with Relativist/Absolutism? He takes a similar approach to Belenky et at. (1986), who argue that there is a position beyond Separated or Connected Knowing which is a synthesis of them both. Belenky et al. call this Constructed Knowing: knowledge is viewed as constructed not received; determined in part by context, not absolute; changeable, not fixed. The values associated with this position are those of social justice and human caring. This synthesis of Separated and Connected perspectives is very similar to Fallibilism, which sees mathematics as a human creation, and is concerned with the social context within which it is embedded and used.

Ernest's Model

Finally, Ernest needs to identify a number of social groups with distinct educational aims. He draws on the work of Williams (1961) and Cosin (1972) to identify five social groups, and he links each with one of the five positions on mathematics education outlined above.

Social Group	Position
Industrial Trainer (New Right)	Dualist/Absolutist
Technological Pragmatist	Multiplistic/Absolutist
Old Humanist	Relativist/Absolutist/Separated
Progressive Educator	Relativist/Absolutist/Connected
Public Educator	Relativist/Fallibilist

The following table is the summary overview used by Ernest in his book.

Social Group	Industrial Trainer	Technological Pragmatist	Old Humanist	Progressive Educator	Public Educator
Political Ideology	Radical Right, 'New Right'	meritocratic, conservative	conservative/liberal	liberal	Democratic socialist
View of Mathematics	Set of Truths and Rules	Unquestioned body of knowledge	Body of structured pure knowledge	Process view: Personalised maths	Social constructivism
Moral Values	Authoritarian 'Victorian' values, Choice, Effort, Self-help, Work, Moral Weakness, Us-good, Them-bad	Utilitarian, Pragmatism, Expediency, 'wealth creation', Technological development	'Blind' Justice, Objectivity, Rule-centred Structure, Hierarchy, Paternalistic 'Classical' view	Person-centred, Caring, Empathy, Human values, Nurturing, Maternalistic, 'Romantic' view	Social Justice, Liberty, Equality, Fraternity, Social awareness, Engagement and Citizenship
Theory of Society	Rigid Hierarchy Market-place	Meritocratic Hierarchy	Elitist, Class stratified	Soft Hierarchy Welfare State	Inequitable hierarchy needing reform
Theory of the Child	Elementary School Tradition: Child 'fallen angel' and 'empty vessel'	Child 'empty vessel' and 'blunt tool' Future worker or manager	Dilute Elementary School view Character building Culture tames	Child-centred, Progressive view, Child: 'growing flower' and 'innocent savage'	Social Conditions view: 'clay moulded by environment' and 'sleeping giant'
Theory of Ability	Fixed and inherited Realized by effort	Inherited ability	Inherited cast of mind	Varies, but needs cherishing	Cultural product: Not fixed

Summary Table from pages 138 and 139 of Ernest (1991)

	'Back-to-Basics': numeracy and social training in obedience	Useful maths to appropriate level and Certification (industry-centred)	Transmit body of mathematical knowledge (Maths-centred)	Creativity, Self-realisation through mathematics (Child-centred)	Critical awareness and democratic citizenship via mathematics
Mathematical Aims					
Theory of Learning	Hard work, effort, practice, rote	Skill acquisition, practical experience	Understanding and application	Activity, Play, Exploration	Questioning, Decision making, Negotiation
Theory of Teaching Mathematics	Authoritarian Transmission, Drill, no 'frills'	Skill instructor Motivate through work-relevance	Explain, Motivate Pass on structure	Facilitate personal exploration Prevent Failure	Discussion, Conflict Questioning of content and pedagogy
Theory of Resources	Chalk and Talk Only Anti-calculator	Hands-on and Microcomputers	Visual aids to motivate	Rich environment to explore	Socially relevant Authentic
Theory of Assessment in Maths	Avoid cheating External testing of simple basics	External tests and certification Skill profiling	External examinations based on hierarchy	Teacher led internal assessment Avoid failure	Various modes. Use of social issues and content
Theory of Social Diversity	Differentiated schooling by Class Crypto-racist, Monoculturalist	Vary curriculum by future occupations	Vary curriculum by ability only (maths neutral)	Humanise neutral maths for all: Use local culture	Accommodation of social and cultural diversity a necessity

Explorations

1. Using the overview table as a guide, describe the theory of society held by each of the five social groups.
2. What is *your* 'theory of ability in mathematics'? Compare it with those of each of the social groups.
3. Use the model to analyse
   (1) the aims of mathematics in the mathematics curriculum,
   (2) some of the current proposals for national assessment and qualifications,
   (3) the approaches used in common mathematics textbooks and teaching resources.
4. Describe the relative influence each of the five social groups has on mathematics education at the moment.
5. Ernest offers a critical review of his model, noting its weaknesses and strengths, on pages 214 - 216 of his book. Summarise this review and discuss the value of the model.
6. Ernest is writing about mathematics education in the United Kingdom. To what extent is his analysis applicable in New Zealand?

References

Belenky, M, Clinchy, B, Goldberger, N and Tarule, J. (1986). *Women's Ways of Knowing: The Development of Self, Voice, and Mind.* New York, Basic Books.

Bishop, A. (1988). *Mathematical Enculturation.* Kluwer Academic Press.

Boston, J, Haig, B and Lauder, H. (1988). The Third Wave: a Critique of the New Zealand Treasury's Report on Education. Part II. *New Zealand Journal of Educational Studies* 23(2), 115-143.

Cosin, B. (1972). *Ideology.* Milton Keynes, Open University.

Ellerton, N and Clements, M. (1994). *The National Curriculum Debacle.* West Australia: Meridian Press.

Erlwanger, S. (1973). Benny's Conception of Rules and Answers in IPI Mathematics. *Journal of Children's Mathematical Behaviour.* 1(2), 7-26.

Ernest, P. (1991). *The Philosophy of Mathematics Education.* The Falmer Press.

Gilligan, C. (1982). *In a Different Voice.* Cambridge, Massachusetts, Harvard University Press.

Lawton, D. (1983). *Curriculum Studies and Educational Planning.*

Hodder and Stoughton.

Neyland, J. (1995a). Teachers' Knowledge: the Starting Point for a Critical Analysis of Mathematics Teaching. In Almeida, D and Ernest, P. (Eds). *Perspectives: Teaching and the Nature of Mathematics*. Exeter University, London.

Neyland, J. (1995b). Neo-behaviourism and Social Constructivism in Mathematics Education. *SAMEpapers 95*. Centre for Science and Mathematics Education Research, University of Waikato.

Perry, W. (1970). *Forms of Intellectual and Ethical Development in the College Years: A Scheme*. New York: Holt, Rinehart and Winston.

Skilbeck, M. (1976). Ideologies and Values; Unit 3 of Course E203. *Curriculum Design and Development*. Milton Keynes, Open University.

Williams, R. (1961). *The Long Revolution*. Harmondsworth, Penguin Books.

Acknowledgement
I am grateful to Taylor and Francis Publishers for giving permission for the use of the table on pages 146 and 147 of this chapter.

15 Cultural Issues in NZ Mathematics Education

Bill Barton

Introduction

New Zealand's response to cultural influences in mathematics education has become a focus of world attention. What is it that is so interesting? This chapter is the personal view of a mathematics teacher who has had the good fortune to be involved in the exciting developments of the last ten years. If, after reading this chapter, you are interested in reading more, try Cocking and Mestre (1988).

How have cultural influences shaped mathematics education in this country? This question presupposes another: *Can* mathematics teaching be influenced by social and cultural factors? Many people view *mathematics* as culture free, but this claim is increasingly disputed (see for example, Bishop, 1988). There is no such debate over the cultural neutrality of *mathematics education*. The teaching and learning of mathematics has never been, and can never be, removed from a consideration of the society in which it takes place. It is not necessary to read theoretical texts on the sociology of education to realise that the missionaries taught mathematics in a different way, and for different reasons, from Kura Kaupapa Maori teachers today. Teachers don't just use Maori kowhaiwhai motifs to teach transformation geometry because they are convenient examples of strip patterns; and the high proportion of non-native speakers of English in Auckland classrooms will inevitably lead to mathematics teachers changing their teaching approaches.

The first half of this chapter describes some of the cultural forces which have shaped mathematics education in NZ. The second half outlines some of the theoretical ideas which have emerged from an examination of this situation, and points out some of the difficulties involved in discussing these complex issues. One growing international field of study of real interest is *ethnomathematics* (the study of cultural

J. Neyland (ed), Mathematics Education: A Handbook for Teachers, Vol.2, 150-164
© *1995 Wellington College of Education: New Zealand*

aspects of mathematics). The research in this field has important implications for mathematics curricula in schools, and for our collective understanding of what mathematics actually is. Studies of the relationship between mathematics and language have led to an examination of bilingualism in mathematics education. Studies of the political dimensions of mathematics education, particularly those involving the emancipation of indigenous people, have led to new understandings of values and control within education. How will our education system cope with these varied, and sometimes conflicting, demands and the resulting power dynamics?

Cultural Forces

NZ's approach to mathematics education is based on the British tradition. During the sixties we were influenced by some American ideas, particularly the New Math revolution, and more recently our mathematics education has developed an antipodean character similar to Australia's. However a simplistic characterisation such as this tends to highlight the similarities between countries and to mask the distinctive features of the NZ system.

Early Days
It would be a mistake to think that mathematics education, even formal mathematics education, began with the missionary schools set up in the early 1800's. Mathematical components were clearly evident in traditional Maori society. These mathematical components were not grouped together as a class of knowledge as they are today, with a name equivalent to mathematics. Counting, measurement, design, navigation, manipulation of shape, and mechanical aids to lifting and movement were an integral part of a life that included building large structures, crafting ocean-going vessels, designing and decorating clothes, homes, furniture and tools (Riini, 1993).

How does this history affect mathematics education now? Firstly, this is not just history. Maori culture continues, and continues to perpetuate itself through formal means. For example, carving schools, weaving courses and marae projects include mathematical aspects which are part of the education system in this country. Those schools which retain Maori character (e.g., the old Native Schools, and today, Kura Kaupapa Maori and Bilingual Schools) retain an ethos in which mathematics is more integrated into other areas of knowledge. In addition, as good teachers have known for a long time, Maori culture offers many examples of mathematical ideas which can be used effectively with NZ children because the concepts are familiar:

kowhaiwhai patterns; woven shapes and designs; the usefulness of naturally occurring curves in design; and the analysis of natural cycles.

It is important to remember this history for another reason too. The dominance of any culture leads to a blindness that things can be otherwise. Over the last twenty-five years there has been a steady push for more integrated studies: to see school mathematics as part of our daily lives and intertwined with other areas of knowledge. In NZ, holistic mathematics education is an old idea. Perhaps we can use this tradition to design a contemporary mathematics education for a technological world.

Maori Mathematics Education
How has mathematics education impinged on Maori children? Has it met their needs? Has it adapted to their presence? What changes have Maori brought about?

Education in NZ has something of an embarrassing history with respect to Maori, and mathematics was an important part of that history. You can find out more about this by reading Shuker (1987), Sharlene Forbes in Volume 1 of this book, and Ohia (1993). The first schools were, of course, set up for Maori, and must have been exclusively Maori in their enrolment. Mathematics (that is, arithmetic) was taught in Maori, and texts were available in Maori until the late 1800's (Taratoa, 1858). There are records of Maori students having an aptitude for the subject and there are accounts of distinctively Maori techniques: the use of song to learn tables, for example (see Knight in Volume 1).

But, as with other subjects, the enforced use of English as the language of instruction, formal examinations, and the use of an imported curriculum caused increasing alienation and a decline in achievement. Success in mathematics often required cutting oneself off from friends and family (Mitchell and Mitchell, 1988). It is not surprising that most Maori children chose not to do that.

An attempt to address this intolerable situation began in the 1970's with the start of the bilingual school movement in primary schools. This extended to secondary schools in the 1980's (Manatu Maori, 1991). An initial mathematics text for primary schools (Rikihana, 1982) was followed by a regular resource-sharing publication called *Te Kupenga* (Barton, 1986). Regular meetings of mathematics teachers of bilingual classes started in 1985. These groups initiated a programme of vocabulary development, a research programme, and other curriculum initiatives (see Maori Language Commission, 1991; Ohia, Moloney and Knight, 1989; Elvin and Trinick, 1987, respectively).

During the last five years there has been an attempt to build on these early developments. A delegation of Maori attended the International Congress on Mathematics Education (Te Puni Kokiri, 1993). There has been further vocabulary development and research (Barton, Fairhall and Trinick, 1995), and more recently a complete curriculum has been written by Maori for Maori as an alternative to the national curriculum (Ministry of Education, 1994). This Maori curriculum has attracted international interest. Nowhere else in the world has an indigenous minority demanded (and received) the right to have an alternative curriculum. It was written using the same resources and time as the standard version. It is published only in the Maori language, and much of the vocabulary and syntax is new.

How is this document different from the standard version? What distinctive features does it have that will contribute to NZ mathematics education more generally? The most notable feature is, not surprisingly, an aspect of the traditional education which has been abandoned with the introduction of a European education system: Maori refer to it as *wairua*. It is an expression of the wholeness, the integrity, the relevance, the spirituality, and the integration of mathematics education. Mathematics is re-imbued with that link with people and purpose so that even the most abstract symbols and relations are experienced as part of one's life. This spirit is present explicitly in the opening section, but also implicitly through the use of Maori language. *Toku reo, toku mapihi pounamu - My language, the means for expression of my inner self.* (Nathan et al., 1993).

Another feature is the focus on the need for learning to be shared and used. An integral part of a statistical survey, for example, is the action which comes from the results: mathematics learning is there to serve the community, not just to serve the needs of the individual.

In addition there are some content features which draw on the Maori way of viewing things. The use of *whakapapa (genealogy)* as an organising principle; the use of particular metaphors for mathematical ideas (e.g., *kauwhata (framework on which fish are dried)* for *graph*) will mean that students learning through this curriculum will develop their mathematical concepts in subtly different ways. As further work is done in the field of ethnomathematics (see below) we can expect these features to increase.

Pacific Island Mathematics Education

NZ has had a significant Pacific Island immigration since the mid-fifties: the population has grown so that Auckland is now the largest Polynesian city in the world. What has this brought to mathematics education?

Pacific Island students who have come to NZ specifically to

become educated expect to study for examination success. They thus support a traditional view of mathematics, and teacher-led approaches to teaching. These students are grounded in the values of their own culture; values such as having an unquestioning respect for elders and teachers. It is not surprising, therefore, that there is a preference for the more traditional transmission mode of teaching which is more common in Pacific Island schools. Pacific Island students have experienced difficulty in those classrooms where the more European values of questioning, doubting, and justifying one's thinking are integral to mathematics learning.

Pacific Island residents of NZ do not experience education within the context of their own culture. They experience social dislocation and alienation in what is, for them, a foreign culture and education system. This alienation has been particularly acute in subjects like mathematics which are perceived to be at the greatest distance from their experience and culture. Attempts to alleviate such difficulties have included the formation of a Pacific Island mathematics teachers' group in Auckland during the mid-1980's, and various initiatives at individual schools, for example, a Samoan bilingual class at Richmond Rd School in Auckland.

In 1992 a UNESCO-funded conference of delegates from seven Pacific Nations was held at Waikato University. Mathematika Pasefika included papers on curricula, vocabulary and resources. A vocabulary database was published along with the proceedings of the conference (Begg, 1991a and b). Waikato University's research centre for mathematics education now hosts several graduate students from Pacific Island countries who have come to study (and contribute to) mathematics education in NZ before returning to home to practise.

Asian Influences
Asian immigration has brought about a relatively new cultural influence on mathematics education in this country, particularly in Auckland. Some schools have reported an increase in Asian students from 5% to nearly 30% in the five-year period since 1988. How does such a changing classroom demography affect a subject like mathematics?

So far there has been little research in this area in NZ, but it is possible to draw on the experiences of other countries. Australia has begun a number of comparative studies (e.g., Bell and Deet, 1993; Bell and Kang, 1994). In Queensland, for example, where there are now a large number of Asian immigrants, Linda Galligan at the University of Southern Queensland, is looking into how mathematics teaching is being affected. In America, which has had a significant Asian population for many years, there have been several studies examining the cultural difference in the teaching and learning of mathematics (e.g., Stigler and Baranes, 1988; Stigler, 1994).

What then, can be said about Asian students and mathematics? What are the issues concerning teachers? What influences are being felt throughout the country? There is a widely believed myth that Asian students are naturally mathematically gifted. This view is largely based on the fact that Asian students perform very well in national examinations, they earn places in mathematics Olympiad teams, and sometimes particular individuals show unusual mathematical brilliance (Tan, for example, completed a degree in Christchurch at age 14). However, there are other factors which must be borne in mind when interpreting these facts. Many Asian immigrants come from selected, high achieving, groups. Education is given priority within Asian culture, and this often results in students showing dedication to their school work and putting in extended periods of study. Thirdly, many Asian students have experienced a schooling system prior to coming to NZ which is different from ours. Stigler describes Chinese and Japanese mathematics classrooms as positive learning environments, strongly focused on content and formal examinations. More time is spent on mathematics learning than in NZ.

Asian students in NZ schools are represented in all grades of mathematics classes, but they do achieve better as a group. It is important to see what we can learn from this. Elaine Mayo, in her chapter in Volume 1, identifies a number of questions which should be asked about underachieving students. We should be asking equivalent questions about these higher achieving students too.

Asian immigration would appear to have caused other indirect effects such as an increased use of private coaching and formal study by the wider NZ community in an attempt to match the examination success achieved by Asian immigrants. Another issue which is being brought to the fore by Asian, and other, immigration patterns is racism in the classroom. Mathematics teachers are increasingly needing to play the role of the social moderator, facing squarely and not condoning racist sentiment in their classrooms.

Non-English Speaking Background Students
Language is a major issue for teachers in mathematics classes with immigrant students of any kind. How do you teach mathematics to a student who cannot understand English? It is now commonplace for teachers to attend courses in techniques which can be used for NESB (Non-English Speaking Background) students. Several books are available on this subject (e.g., Bickmore-Brand, 1990; Houston, 1989).

Some institutions offer introductory courses for NESB students. The
School of Mathematical and Information Science at the University of
Auckland, for example, runs a special course for intending NESB
students. The identification of language as an important factor in
mathematics learning has led to some of the second-language techniques being used in mathematics classes. But it has also highlighted
the significance of mathematics itself as a language.

The language issues associated with NESB students has also caused
mathematics educators to re-examine the goals of mathematics
education. In one instance, an engineering course required students to
have high marks in bursary mathematics. This resulted in a high
proportion of students with difficulty communicating in English being
accepted. The course supervisors began to question the validity of
formal examinations as a way of assessing the kind of mathematical
ability which was required for their course. These and other similar
experiences are causing educators to revisit questions such as: What
mathematics and mathematical skills are required for further scien-
tific/technical education? Are these the same as those needed for pure
mathematics or for a general mathematical education? Does the school
mathematics curriculum and its assessment procedures meet these
needs?

Theoretical Issues

It is difficult to summarise the influences particular cultures make to
NZ society because such summaries must include generalisations, and
generalisations can easily become stereotypes. It is perhaps preferable
to describe cultural interaction in mathematics education in a general
way, and to illustrate this with examples from particular cultures. This
is the approach I shall take in what follows.

However even this type of analysis has its problems. The main
problem is that the dominant culture (in this case European middle-
class NZ) becomes a reference-point or a norm, in relation to which all
other cultures are compared. Such an ethnocentric bias is inevitable
because writers cannot escape their own experience. One solution
would be to have parallel presentations illustrating the points of view
of other cultures. In lieu of that, the best I can do here is to acknowledge the problem and to try to point out where it is particularly
intrusive. I have chosen three issues for discussion: ethnomathematics,
language, and cultural politics.

Ethnomathematics

The international literature on ethnomathematics has burgeoned since questions were raised during the mid-eighties about the extent to which mathematics education is influenced by social and cultural factors. Educators began to realise that these factors played a more significant role than previously acknowledged. The literature does not concur on the definition of ethnomathematics, except that it concerns mathematics and culture. Much of this writing is about the mathematical practices of particular ethnic or social groups. Pam Harris (1991), for example, discusses Australian aboriginal conceptions of space, time and money, and there has been an investigation of the mathematics of street children in Brazil (Carraher and Schliemann 1990). Ascher (1993) discusses similar issues.

However, defining ethnomathematics as the mathematical practices of cultural or social groups leads to some problems. It is almost certain that no-one will find a 'mathematics' of equal sophistication to the 'mathematics' which is taught in most classrooms around the world. Ethnomathematics so defined is doomed to be a poor relation to mathematics, and will only be of interest as a curiosity, or at most, as a motivating factor for some children. An alternative is to define ethnomathematics as the study of the mathematical aspects of the ideas and practices of cultural or social groups. In this way no attempt is being made to define the mathematics of, say, the Maori - and thus no invidious comparisons can be made. This definition also reflects the fact that traditional Maori culture did not include a subject category equivalent to mathematics, and so it is inappropriate to create one.

Having established that we are interested in the mathematical ideas and practices of particular groups, it is useful to distinguish between surface features and conceptual features. Surface features which exhibit mathematical concepts include such things as basket designs, navigational techniques, counting words, and measuring instruments. They are interesting socially as well as mathematically because they represent different ways of doing things. Such features are useful in mathematics education as resources from which interest can be created and new experiences derived.

Conceptual features of a culture reflect underlying understandings of relations, shapes, and number. These deep-seated cultural forms are exhibited in the language and logic used to describe mathematical ideas, and the way such ideas are used to interpret the real world.

It is important to realise that just because a particular mathematical concept is different, does not make it wrong or primitive. Nor is it a problem if a mathematical concept is expressed using metaphorical language. Some people doubt the value of mathematical ideas being expressed in this way, yet everyone, whatever their culture, learns through metaphor, and has their concepts shaped by them. As an example, compare the concept of 'solution' formed by students who have balanced an algebraic equation, with that which will be held by students using new graphical technology. The former think of the solution as a number which causes the equation to balance; the latter 'see' it as a point of intersection of two lines.

It is not being suggested that these ideas and practices of cultural groups are mathematics - they are ideas from other sources which we identify as having mathematical characteristics. So far as mathematics education is concerned, they are useful because they can contribute to curriculum design; that is, they can be used to introduce mathematics in ways which are congruent to the group in question.

How has ethnomathematics contributed to mathematics education in NZ? It is obvious from my earlier remarks that some aspects of Maori culture have become part of our curriculum: kowhaiwhai patterns are a common resource for the introduction of ideas of transformation geometry, for example. But how can the values and deeper relational concepts also become part of mathematics education? One important example is the way that whakapapa (genealogy) is being used to teach, explain and develop Maori mathematics vocabulary - and thus to teach mathematics. In the early days of vocabulary development it was important that the words selected help understanding rather than present a new item to be learnt. It was realised that if base words could be built upon to form vocabulary for more complex terms, then mathematics learning could go hand-in-hand with vocabulary learning. It has turned out that this idea of a whakapapa of vocabulary has been particularly useful in explaining the new vocabulary to Maori elders - who have thus been taught mathematics using their own conceptual structures.

Pacific Island resources are used in mathematics in the same way as Maori designs, but deeper cultural concepts are not yet evident in NZ mathematics education. It may be that, in the future, the oral Pacific culture has some components which will contribute to new perspectives on mathematics.

The Asian influence is largely unresearched beyond the sociology of the classroom. Some researchers are looking at the ways different cultural groups form the conception of number (Bell, 1990). It appears likely that different approaches to teaching lead to different conceptions of mathematics. For example there is a perception that Asian students favour a more rule-bound, formal mathematics. But caution is necessary. If true, this assertion may be a result of different cultural conceptions - but it could also be a result of English language difficulties, or of the selection of students who come to this country. This would be an interesting area for future research.

Language

The presence in NZ classrooms of languages other than English has focused attention on the language aspects of mathematics education. This focus has been an international phenomenon of increasing importance, and previously monolingual countries (like NZ) have much to learn. Language studies have resulted in three major areas of investigation: bilingual mathematics education; mathematics as a language; and the impact of NESB (non-English speaking background) students in mathematics classes.

The growth of mathematics education in Maori has already been mentioned. Not only has the development of a Maori mathematics vocabulary provided another metaphorical base for the subject, but also Maori words are being more widely adopted as part of a general mathematics education. For example the official curriculum document suggests that young children learn to count first in Maori, since the structure of that language's counting words is more explicitly base ten than in English. Another example is the common use of the Patiki number sequence to complement the triangular and square number sequences.

Samoan/English bilingual classes also exist, and it remains to be seen what contributions that language will make. As this and other Pacific and Asian languages become more commonly spoken by students within their mathematics lessons it is likely that the structure of these languages themselves will provide mathematical perspectives not presently available to monolingual English speakers. Research and theory emanating from Canada and elsewhere (e.g., Cummins and Swain, 1986) state that the process of using more than one language to express mathematical ideas is additive in itself. That is, given sufficient proficiency in both languages, students are liable to have better understanding because they have two modes in which to think and communicate. If this is correct, then the introduction of bilingualism into our mathematics education will alone improve the standard of the mathematics.

A second contribution of languages other than English in mathematics education is the heightened awareness of the extent to which learning mathematics is like learning a language. This is, of course, by no means the whole of mathematics learning. However some teachers have begun to use this idea as a supplement to their teaching in totally English-speaking classes. Techniques from language teaching such as split information tasks, vocabulary maintenance, and communication tasks have been designed for use in mathematics. For example, the several lines of an algebraic solution of an equation can be written on separate pieces of paper, both in words and in symbols. Each of these is given to a different student. They then work together to reconstruct the solution without showing their pieces of paper. Further examples can be found in MacGregor and Moore (1991) and Hill and Edwards (1991). Once this idea is established it is possible to use other languages with students who do not speak them. The task of communicating in a foreign mode has the effect of forcing clarification of mathematical concepts.

In many parts of NZ it is now common for mathematics teachers to participate in courses designed to help them teach NESB students. Some courses have been run especially for mathematics teachers. On the students' side, there have been courses for NESB students taking mathematics. These courses introduce the particular language characteristics of mathematics. Mathematics discourse has distinct features not found in normal English. For example, it is particularly dense, it is very precise, it is read in multiple directions (not just from left to right), and it contains familiar words with precise meanings which are different from their normal meanings (e.g., in mathematics 'or' often means 'one or the other or both'). More importantly for NESB students, the participles and connectives are extremely important in carrying the exact meaning of the sentence. If you wish to explore the relationship between language, mathematics and teaching, Stephens et al. (1993) is a good place to start.

Cultural Politics

A third aspect of culture in mathematics education is the political influence of particular cultures. The recent Maori renaissance and the accompanying developments in mathematics education (outlined above) have caused a re-examination of many national institutions. What would be the consequence of the Maori community dismissing national examinations in mathematics as inappropriate for Kura Kaupapa Maori students? Where would that leave the students? What kind of mathematics education would be appropriate? What are the criteria by which an alternative mathematics education would be recognised as equally significant for further education and employment? People are questioning the structures which have led to the indigenous cultural group being disadvantaged. The new Maori mathematics curriculum is only the beginning of a new way forward. The complete curriculum delivery and evaluation system must also be modified.

The Pacific Island political agenda also has roots in the elevation of their cultures, but these communities are at a disadvantage because they are not indigenous to this country. How can they question a system which discriminates against them? In a reversal of NZ's past colonial influence on Pacific Nations, we are now starting to see mathematics education with a Pacific character coming into NZ. This will not be achieved without resistance in NZ. This adjustment of power relationships is a good example of the politics of mathematics education.

The Asian political influence is more economically based. There are large numbers of students from China, Korea, Taiwan and Hong Kong coming to NZ to gain qualifications which are not as accessible in their own countries. Many of these students (and their parents) are professionally oriented, and they demand an education which will maximise their opportunities for careers in commerce, medicine, engineering and so on. Because a significant proportion of these students are paying for their courses, education institutions in NZ are responding by shifting the emphasis towards exam-preparation, and towards vocation-oriented mathematics courses. Those institutions providing such courses are likely to have increasing influence on education policy because of their growth in size and financial resources. This is an example of the educational values and practices characteristic of a particular community influencing the wider group.

This sort of realignment of power relations leads to some difficult questions. To what extent can such moves be controlled? If they can be controlled, should they be moderated? Is there a reverse influence towards those countries who receive our graduates? How do we deal with opposing values within mathematics education? In a situation where we have conflicting values in mathematics education what is meant by phrases like "improve mathematics learning", "the best mathematics education available", "standards have increased"?

The interaction between cultures has led to an increased awareness of the politics of mathematics education. This in turn has led to a renewed examination of the fundamental aims of mathematics teaching. That in itself must be counted as a positive influence from the increasing cultural diversity of our nation.

The Future

Looking at cultural influences in mathematics education through the constructs of ethnomathematics, language and politics highlights the way in which mathematics education is determined predominantly by a European NZ culture. The more that other cultures are allowed to express themselves through education the more we will become aware of other perspectives on mathematics. The experiences students have in mathematics classrooms are likely, therefore, to become richer. This richness will not just be because other languages, resources, techniques and contexts are brought into the lessons. It will also be richer because teachers and students will both become more aware of the limitations of a monocultural viewpoint, and will therefore seek other perspectives which may prove to be mathematically valuable, as well as interesting in themselves and motivating for those students whose cultures are represented.

References

Ascher, Marcia (1993). *Ethnomathematics: A Multicultural View of Mathematical Ideas.* Belmont, CA: Brooks/Cole Publishing Co.

Barton, B. (1986). *Te Kupenga.* Auckland: Mathematics Education Centre Auckland (MECA), Auckland College of Education.

Barton, B., Fairhall, U., and Trinick, T. (1995). A History of the Development of Maori Mathematics Vocabulary. *SAMEpapers 1995.*

Begg, A. J. C. (1991a). *Mathematika Pasefika: Vocabulary Database.* Hamilton: Centre for Science and Mathematics Education Research.

Begg, A. J. C. (1991b). *Mathematika Pasefika: Conference Proceedings* Hamilton: Centre for Science and Mathematics Education Research.

Bell, G. (1990). Language and Counting: Some Recent Results. In *Mathematics Education Research Journal,* 2(1) 1-14.

Bell, G. and Deet, C. (eds) (1993). *Asian Perspectives on Mathematics Education.* Canberra: Northern Rivers Mathematical Association.

Bell, G. and Kang Ok-Ki (1994). Constraints on the Intended Curriculum in Australia and Korea. In *Proceedings of MERGA-17 Conference,* Vol 1. Lismore: Mathematics Education Research Group Australasia.

Bickmore-Brand, J. (ed) (1990). *Language in Mathematics.* Victoria, Australia: Australian Reading Association.

Bishop, A. J. (1988). *Mathematical Enculturation: A Cultural Perspective on Mathematics Education.* Dordrecht: Kluwer Academic Publishers.

Carraher, T. N., Carraher, D. W. and Schliemann A. D. (1985). Mathematics in the Street and in Schools. *British Journal of Developmental Psychology,* 3, 21-29.

Cocking, R. R. and Mestre, J. P. (eds) (1988). *Linguistic and Cultural Influences on Learning Mathematics.* Hillsdale, N.J.: Erlbaum.

Cummins, J. and Swain, M (1986). *Bilingualism in Education: Aspects of Research, Theory and Practice.* Harlow, U.K.: Longman.

Elvin, K. and Trinick, T. (1987). *Nga Mauranga.* Auckland: Mathematics Education Centre Auckland (MECA), Auckland College of Education.

Harris, P. (1991). *Mathematics in a Cultural Context.* Geelong: Deakin University.

Hill, S and Edwards, F. (1991). *Language and Learning in Secondary Schools: Mathematics.* Wellington: Ministry of Education, Learning Media.

Houston, C. (1989). *English Language Development Across the Curriculum.* Queensland: Immigration Education Service.

MacGregor, M. and Moore, R. (1991). *Teaching Mathematics in the Multicultural Classroom.* Melbourne: The University of Melbourne.

Manatu Maori (1991). *E Tipu, E Rea: Maori Education - Current Status.* Wellington: Ministry of Maori Affairs.

Maori Language Commission (1991). *Nga Kupu Tikanga Pangarau - Mathematics Vocabulary.* Wellington: Learning Media.

Ministry of Education (1994). *Draft Maori Mathematics Curriculum.* Wellington: Ministry of Education.

Mitchell, H. A. and Mitchell, M. J. (1988). *Profiles of Maori Pupils with High Marks in School Certificate English and Mathematics.* Nelson: Mitchell Research.

Nathan, G., Trinick, T., Tobin, E. and Barton, B. (1993). Tahi Rua, Toru, Wha: Mathematics Counts in Maori Renaissance. In Stephens et al. (eds)*Communicating Mathematics: Perspectives from Classroom Practice and Current Research.* Hawthorn: ACER.

Ohia, M., Moloney, M. and Knight, G. (1989). *Mathematics Education in Secondary Bilingual Units.* Palmerston North: Massey University.

Ohia, M. (1993). Adapting Mathematics to meet Maori Needs and Aspirations: An Attempt to Shift Paradigms. *SAMEpapers 1993,* 104-115.

Riini, M. and Riini, S. (1993). Historical Perspectives of Maori Mathematics. In Te Puni Kokiri *Pangarau - Maori Mathematics and Education.* 17-21.

Rikihana, T. (1982). *Mathematics.* Auckland: Auckland College of Education.

Shuker, R. (1987). *The One Best System? A Revisionist History of State Schooling in New Zealand.* Palmerston North: Dunmore Press.

Stephens, M., Waywood, A., Clarke, D. and Izard, J. (1994). *Communicating Mathematics: Perspectives from Classroom Practice and Current Research.* Hawthorn, Australia: Australian Council for

Educational Research.

Stigler, J. and Baranes, R. (1988). Culture and Mathematics Learning. In *Review of Research in Education*, 15, 253-305.

Stigler, J. (1994). Learning Mathematics from Classroom Instruction: Cross-Cultural and Experimental Perspectives. Keynote Address, MERGA-17 Conference, Lismore.

Taratoa, H (1858). *Maori Arithmetic Book for Schools*. Unknown.

Te Puni Kokiri (1993). *Pangarau - Maori Mathematics and Education*. Wellington: Ministry of Maori Development.

16   The Politics of Mathematics Education

Bill Barton

Introduction

Mathematics? Political? Surely Not?
Education is a social endeavour, and few would deny that it has a political component. The battles reflected in newspaper columns, the disputes between teachers and government offices, and the arguments in court about the running of schools are all evidence of the strength of feeling and the lengths to which people will go to obtain an educational system which they believe is best.

However, although we take all those debates as inevitable, it is less clear that mathematics education, in particular, has political aspects separate from, say, English education, early childhood education, or Maori education. This chapter argues that, not only is mathematics education deeply political in ways which are specific to the subject, but also that it is one of the most political of all subjects.

The New Zealand Experience
The situation in New Zealand during the last twenty years has clearly illustrated both the educational and the cultural politics of mathematics. Educational politics are intensified in a social environment in which jobs are not freely available, and where therefore, the gatekeeping function of schools is more important than ever. Mathematics achievement has always been a prime means of gatekeeping and a criterion for academic advancement. In some areas, ability in mathematics is virtually synonymous with intelligence, creating an artificial elevation of the importance of this subject.

Furthermore the shift towards a market ideology in New Zealand education has brought about changes in who controls the curriculum and who runs educational organisations. The latest Achievement Initiative has been spearheaded by mathematics: it was the first subject

J. Neyland (ed), Mathematics Education: A Handbook for Teachers, Vol.2, 165-174
© *1995 Wellington College of Education: New Zealand*

to have its curriculum rewritten, and the arguments over the politics of that process were played out for the first time between mathematics teachers, mathematics educators, and the Ministry of Education.

Cultural politics are also visible in mathematics. The Maori renaissance of the last twenty years has brought into focus the cultural nature of our curriculum, and has for the first time, challenged the English legacy of our schools. It is interesting that, of all subjects, mathematics was the first to form bilingual teachers' groups, produce bicultural resources, and develop a technical Maori vocabulary. It was one such group that instigated the Maori-language mathematics curriculum contract to parallel the English-language document (Ministry of Education, 1992 and 1994), and thereby established the need for bicultural curricula at all levels. The precedent has been set. Now all subjects which will have parallel Maori curriculum documents.

Two Aspects of the Politics of Mathematics Education
For the purposes of this chapter it is helpful to consider two broad areas in which mathematics education has a political impact.

The first is at the level of the classroom or school system. This relates both to the way mathematics is part of the gatekeeping process in our society, and to the way it is part of a national education system which functions in a social environment. Classroom politics refers to the way in which those in control (usually teachers) carry out the intended and the hidden mathematics curriculum. This is gate*keeping*. But teachers work within a curriculum and a school environment which is only partly under their control. In other words, while teachers keep the gates, those gates are constructed by others. The politics of gate*making* take place in the regional and national education institutions.

The second area is the politics of culture and relates to the way in which mathematics itself is part of the way we live our lives. Mathematics as an academic subject carries particular values, and being educated into mathematics can be seen as being "enculturated into the culture of mathematics" (Bishop, 1988). Questions can be asked about how these values are set, who validates them, how are they passed on, and who benefits from them. The values of mathematics, particularly the rational paradigm it sets, pervade our society in ways that are more deep-seated than first seems. In a very real sense those who control these values are power-brokers.

There is an international aspect to this second area of mathematical politics. In so far as mathematical values characterise the way a society conducts itself, these values are important in the international relations of that society. This is particularly noticeable in imperial/colonial relations where, through education, trade and force of arms, one society gains and retains power over another. Historically, it can be seen in European colonisation of Africa and the Pacific, and perhaps we are seeing it again in the contemporary rise of multi-national companies in world economics? Mathematics has a stronger role in this process than has previously been acknowledged (Bishop, 1990).

The Politics of School Mathematics

Mathematics and Gatekeeping

It is an interesting phenomenon that, although the amount of recognisable, school mathematics actually performed by people at home or in their work is very small, this subject is one of the greatest determinants of vocational or educational advancement.

Studies both in New Zealand (Knight, 1993) and overseas (Harris M, 1991) into the mathematics needed in non-specialised vocations and in day-to-day living have revealed that there is very little content which is absolutely necessary. We are now recognising that what is required in the quantitative domain are analytic processes and some statistical skills rather than content. Nevertheless the mathematics which is contained in the examinations that give entrée to further education or to jobs, does not match well with identified practical needs. Whoever solved a quadratic equation by factorisation, outside of a school classroom? When was it necessary to prove a trigonometric identity, or factor a number greater than 100? Even the practical skills like using protractors and drawing symmetric designs are more relevantly taught in art, design or technical courses.

It is this dichotomy between the need for mathematics and the requirement for mathematics qualifications which has allowed some successful people in our society to be open about their lack of mathematical ability - it is still socially acceptable to admit to having done poorly in school mathematics, while it is less acceptable to admit to poor English. The fact that these people have circumvented the mathematical "gate" to success does not mean that the gate is not there; but it does raise the question as to whether it is really necessary.

So how has this situation come about? Part of the answer is historical and part is psychological. D'Ambrosio (1992) briefly describes the phases in mathematics education. It has origins in maintaining class distinctions in Greek and early European times, and was adapted during the industrial revolution where some practical mathematics became included in a classic education. There is now a 'mathematics for all' ethos in education. New Zealand, with its avowedly egalitarian colonial history, nevertheless used education, and mathematics, to maintain class and vocational distinctions. An example was the double streams of academic and vocational mathematics taught in secondary schools in the 40's and 50's, another is the gender differences in the availability and delivery of mathematics. What questions might we want to ask about the NZ Mathematics Certificate courses today?

The psychology of mathematics in gatekeeping derives from the congruence between theories of mathematics and intelligence on the one hand, and theories of mathematics and rationality on the other. Educational theory became dominated by psychology in America in the first half of this century. This led to "measures" of intelligence and a climate of testing in which mathematics, as an easily "measurable" subject featured strongly. Being good at mathematics became understood as being intelligent: how many times have you heard: "Oh, she's doing maths, she must be bright"? It has been suggested that the double meaning of the word 'rational' - either 'logical' or 'sane' - has influenced our feelings about mathematics. To risk failing at mathematics may be to risk being labelled insane (Ocean, 1994). No wonder mathematics is seen as a powerful force in social relations, and people admit to dropping out, rather than to continuing and failing (or they brag about failing as a defence mechanism which diminishes its importance by ridicule).

Who, it is important to ask, is in control of judging ability in mathematics? Who determines a student's chances of success in the subject? Who has the power to control students' behaviour by threats of failure in this subject, failure which will determine how successful and how "sensible" they are seen to be in society? The mathematics teacher. Is it any wonder that large groups of students have an inordinate fear of the subject? To what extent is this fear a result of justified anticipation that they will be marked for life?

There is then, more than normal teacher power being exerted when a teacher favours some students over others in a mathematics classroom, or when they select a mode of teaching or assessment which will discriminate amongst students, or when they make streaming decisions. As teachers we exert this power whether we are conscious of it or not. What safe-guards can we take in this situation?

Mathematics Curriculum Development - Making the Gates
In New Zealand over the last decade there have been increasing numbers of statements about the control a particular group has over the mathematics curriculum. Whether it is the teachers complaining about the central decision-making of the Ministry; the Business Round Table accusing liberal mathematics educators of capturing education;

government blaming falling standards on teachers' lack of accountability; or parents demanding entry into schools they perceive to be 'better' - one group perceives a particular coterie as having control over something which concerns everybody.

The point is that, whatever way the control is exercised, even if it is shared, there will always be an identifiable group which has some form of control over the mathematics curriculum. This means that there will always be a set of questions which constantly need to be asked and examined. Questions like:

- Who has control over what aspects of the curriculum?
- What other groups have influence on the controlling group?
- Whose interests are being served by the mathematics curriculum?
- Whose interests are *not* being served?
- Who is complaining of powerlessness, and why?
- What is the mechanism of curriculum change?
- What is the effect on the individual of the present curriculum?
- What is the effect on society of the present curriculum?

In this context curriculum has its wide meaning: content, resources, teaching and assessment processes. Thus, in the recent past, it is not just the politics of the writing of *Mathematics in the New Zealand Curriculum* (Ministry of Education, 1992) which is of interest, but the whole Achievement Initiative brought in by the 1987-95 National Government, the rise of the New Zealand Qualifications Authority and its National Framework for assessment, and to take an even wider perspective, the relations with similar developments in England, America and Australia.

Mathematics was the first subject to be developed in the Achievement Initiative of Lockwood Smith's era, and so the politics of curriculum control were played out more strongly as different groups sought to gain their place in the total process of curriculum change. This was reflected in the convening of a meeting of many mathematics educators prior to letting the curriculum contract; the mass sacking of the first Advisory group appointed to oversee the writing of the mathematics document; submissions by the Education Forum (a subcommittee of the Business Round Table); threatened walk-outs of the group responsible for the NZQA mathematics Unit Standards; national meetings of Maori educators to determine the process by which a Maori curriculum might be established; significant Ministry of Maori Development funding, Kura Kaupapa Maori and Maori Language Commission interest in mathematics education; and the contemporaneous rise of mathematics educators in university Mathematics Departments.

All this activity in the period 1990-1994 can hardly be coincidence. Mathematics was the board on which changes in curriculum development were played out. For example, it could be argued that the market ideology has become integrated into the mathematics curriculum: that the idea of mathematics education as a subject of general worth within an educated society has given ground to the idea of mathematics education as a skill to be gained and exploited in the vocation market. However, liberal influences are still to be seen in the curriculum document itself. The return of teacher unions and mathematics associations to the arena, and battles still being fought out within NZQA show that the power games continue, and that cycles of influence will persist.

In New Zealand there has been little attempt to analyse the curriculum process in these terms. The flurry of activity detailed above generated reactive accounts of what was happening (Neyland, 1994; Marshall, 1994). The other period of change in recent times - the implementation of New Maths in the 1960's - was documented by Openshaw (1993). A new project, the Mathematics Curriculum Change Longitudinal Investigation, being established in the Mathematics Education Unit of The University of Auckland has exactly this long-term analysis of the process and determinants of change on the mathematics curriculum as its aim (Ellis and Pfannkuch, 1994).

But it is important that all sections of society ask the questions detailed above. What are the answers to them now? How are they different from the early 1990's? What do you predict the answers will be in five years time?

The Politics of a Mathematical Society

The idea that mathematics carries a particular set of social values has only recently been the subject of attention. Questions about mathematics and society only became widely debated in the 1980's, although some earlier books can now be seen to be addressing this issue (Kline, 1953; Bronowski, 1973; Wilder, 1981). The Western legacy of Greek thinking was carried through mathematics. Philosophically it was thought that mathematical truths were the epitome of culture-free, pure thought - truths which could not be doubted. But this century, as mathematics came to be seen as more uncertain (Kline, 1980), it has come to be regarded as a social system. That is, the way mathematics develops in fact is only one of a number of possible lines of development, and the reasons for this particular development are based on needs and values expressed within society.

Because mathematics is a social system we can influence its

development. Political questions arise, therefore, over who influences mathematics, how it is influenced, and how these influences are transmitted to others.

Establishing Mathematical Values
The sociology of mathematics, and of mathematics education, includes the task of uncovering who, in the past, has influenced mathematics, and how and why. Why, for example, was mathematics so closely associated with philosophy in Greek society, and why were those people regarded so highly in that society? What mathematical developments from Asia and the Arab empire were ignored or subsumed into European mathematics, and why did this happen? In what ways did Renaissance trade and commercial pre-occupations affect the type of mathematics which developed and the mathematical schools which emerged at that time? And so on.

Similar questions need to be asked in the present. When these questions involve the power relations between the people concerned, then they are political questions. Who controls the directions in which mathematics develops? What is the relationship between the university mathematicians and economists, military and space scientists, social statisticians, weavers or engineers? How do the values represented in these areas get carried over into mathematics? Would mathematics 'feel' different if it was regarded as more of an Arts subject than a Science one - as it used to be in 18th century Europe. Is it now becoming a Commerce subject? If so, how is that movement occurring?

Mathematical thinking is regarded as systematic, logical and liable to lead to 'the truth'. Is this type of thinking moving into new areas? For example, studies like history, sociology, and education are now labelled 'Social Sciences'. This implies that 'scientific' thinking should be dominant in their development. Do you agree with that? What other alternatives are there?

There have been a few attempts to specify exactly what cultural values are carried within mathematics (Wilder, 1981; Bishop, 1990), but very little, so far, on how these are specific to particular cultures. The values have been described as male (Walkerdine, 1989), and Western European (Bishop, 1990), and some authors have attempted to describe alternative values carried in mathematical activities of other cultures. This latter work is part of a new field known as ethnomathematics (see Ascher, 1991, D'Ambrosio and Ascher, 1994; Gerdes, 1994; Harris P, 1991).

Disseminating Mathematical Values

Mathematics education comes into this picture as the means by which mathematical values are disseminated. Mathematics teachers worldwide (indeed most teachers of most subjects) do not regard their job as inculcating particular values or political stances. But this does not make what has gone on for centuries any less political.

The question of dissemination can be thought of at an individual level, and on a wider scale. On an individual level, political questions can be asked about the interests served by the kind of mathematics education available in schools. Does it empower learners? Is it useful for them? Does it equally support students who will be farmers, bank clerks, labourers, home-keepers and doctors? Does it equally enhance the life-styles of each cultural group? Does it equally support the interests of men and women? Similar questions need to be asked about the way mathematics is taught as well as its content. If the answer is "No" to any of these questions, then how are the differences justified (given that a large part of everyone's educational resources go into this compulsory school subject)? A reference for those interested in this aspect of mathematical politics is *Schools, Mathematics and Work*, (Harris M, 1991).

On a wider scale, it has been claimed (Bishop, 1990) that mathematics has been part of the mechanism by which colonisation takes place. Power is exerted by one country (one culture) over others through trade, administration and education. In particular, mathematical training in colonial situations has been organised in such a way that these three processes function in the mode of the dominant culture: for example, mathematics courses aimed at developing commercial skills.

Developing a theory to explore and counter such action (whether it be conscious or not), is part of current writing in this field. For example, Paulo Freire's theories of critical education, i.e., education for political action and freedom, are now becoming the basis for work in mathematics education (see Mellin-Olsen, 1987; Frankenstein, 1989; Skovsmose, 1994).

Bishop had Europe's colonisation of Africa and the East in mind, but it would be instructive to ask some hard questions about the effect of New Zealand national mathematics examinations in the Pacific over the last thirty years. Whose culture was being promoted, and to what end? By having our school curriculum taught in Pacific nations was it more likely that the top students would come into our tertiary institutions and retain links with our economy, our educational ethos, and our world view? How many of the Pacific's political leaders were educated in this country? What effect does that now have on our international relations?

These are, of course, general educational questions. But mathematics, it must be remembered, is the prime gatekeeper in this situation.

Bishop's argument is that it carries Western European values of objectivity, rationalism and control. A person educated in mathematics comes to value things and events as dehumanised, causally related in discoverable ways, and needing to be controlled. Put like this, it is easy to see that there are alternatives. What balance of values should we have in our society, and what is the role of mathematics education in making that come about?

Summary

It is now accepted by many mathematicians, philosophers and educators that mathematics is not the acultural carrier of ultimate truth that was previously thought. Mathematics can carry values, and it may be promoted to the advantage of particular groups.

It has become one of the most powerful of all school subjects, possibly because of its apparent objectivity. That in itself makes it important to ask who controls the exercise of mathematics, and the means by which it is passed on - that is, mathematics education.

From the classroom teacher, to those interested in international trade, various groups have an interest in what mathematics is taught, and who such teaching is aimed at. It is the province of the politics of mathematics education to expose and analyse the relationships between these groups, and their effect on individuals.

Invisible political forces are powerful. Mathematics education has seemed the least political of all branches of education. It is vital that we recognise its importance.

References

Ascher, M. (1991). *Ethnomathematics: A Multicultural View of Mathematical Ideas*. New York: Brooks/Cole Publishing Co.

Bishop, A. J. (1988). *Mathematical Enculturation: A Cultural Perspective on Mathematics Education*. Dordrecht: Kluwer Academic Publishers.

Bishop, A. J. (1990). Western Mathematics: the Secret Weapon of Cultural Imperialism, in *Race and Class*, 32(2) 51-65.

Bronowski, J. (1973). *The Ascent of Man*. London: Science Horizons Inc.

D'Ambrosio, U. (1985). Ethnomathematics and its place in the History and Pedagogy of Mathematics. *For the Learning of Mathematics* 5(1).

D'Ambrosio, U. and Ascher, M. (1994). Ethnomathematics: A Dialogue. In *For the Learning of Mathematics*, 14(2) 36-43.

Ellis, J. and Pfannkuch, M. (1994). Mathematics Curriculum Change Longitudinal Investigation: Report of Work in Progress. Presented to NZARE Conference, Christchurch, 1994.

Frankenstein, M. (1989). *Relearning Mathematics: A Different Third R - Radical Math*. London: Free Association Books.

Gerdes, P. (1994). Reflections on Ethnomathematics. In *For the Learning of Mathematics*, 14(2), 19-22.

Harris, M. and Evans, J. (1991). Mathematics and Workplace Research. In M. Harris (ed) *Schools, Mathematics and Work*. London: Falmer Press.

Harris, M. (ed) (1991). *Schools, Mathematics and Work*. London: Falmer Press.

Harris, P. (1991). *Mathematics in a Cultural Context*. Geelong: Deakin University.

Kline, M. (1953). *Mathematics in Western Culture*. Oxford: Oxford University Press.

Kline, M. (1980). *Mathematics: The Loss of Certainty*. New York: Oxford University Press.

Knight, G., Arnold, G., Carter, M., Kelly, P. and Thornley, G. (1994). *The Mathematical Needs of New Zealand School Leavers*. Palmerston North: Department of Mathematics, Massey University.

Mellin-Olsen, S. (1987). *The Politics of Mathematics Education*. Dordrecht: Kluwer.

Marshall, J. (ed) (1994). *Revisitng the 'Reforms' in Education*. Auckland: Faculty of Education, The University of Auckland.

Ministry of Education (1993). *Mathematics in the New Zealand Curriculum*. Wellington: Learning Media.

Ministry of Education (1994). *Draft Maori Mathematics Curriculum*. Wellington: Learning Media.

Neyland, J. (1994). Politics, Power, Action Research, and the Social Constructivist Curriculum *Proceedings of MERGA-7*, Southern Cross University, Lismore.

Ocean, J. (1994). Rational, Normal and Sane - The Total Mathematician. Unpublished paper, The University of Auckland.

Openshaw, R. (1993). New Zealand Secondary Schools and the Coming of the New Maths. In *NZ Mathematics Magazine* 29(3) 47-57.

Skovsmose, O. (1994). *Towards a Philosophy of Critical Mathematics Education*. Kluwer Academic Publishers.

Walkerdine, V. (1989). *Counting Girls Out*. Virago.

Wilder, R. L. (1981). *Mathematics as a Cultural System*. Oxford: Pergamon.

Notes on Contributors

Bill Barton is a Lecturer in Mathematics Education at The University of Auckland.

Andy Begg is a Senior Lecturer in Mathematics Education at the Centre for Science, Mathematics and Technology Education Research at the University of Waikato.

Thora Blithe is a Senior Lecturer in Mathematics at Victoria University of Wellington.

Murray Britt is Director of the Centre for Mathematics Education at the Auckland College of Education.

Megan Clark is an Associate Professor in Statistics and Mathematics Education, Victoria University of Wellington.

Bronwen Cowie is Head of Mathematics at Waikato Diocesan School, Hamilton.

Sharleen Forbes is The Manager, Public Policy, Statistics-New Zealand.

Joanna Higgins is a Senior Lecturer in Mathematics Education at the Wellington College of Education.

Lindsay Johnston is a Senior Lecturer in Mathematics at Victoria University of Wellington.

Jane McChesney is a Senior Lecturer, Mathematics Education, School of Education, University of Waikato.

Carol Mayers is a Senior Lecturer in Mathematics Education in the Centre for Mathematics Education at the Auckland College of Education.

Elaine Mayo is an Advisor in Mathematics Education in the Education Advisory Service at the Christchurch College of Education.

Jim Neyland is a Lecturer in Mathematics Education in the Mathematics and Science Education Centre at Victoria University of Wellington.

Roger Openshaw is a Senior Lecturer in the Department of Policy Studies in Education at Massey University.

Stan Roberts is a retired member of the former Applied Mathematics Division of the DSIR.

Liz Stone is a Mathematics Advisor in the Education Advisory Service, Auckland College of Education.

Kerry Taylor is a Mathematics Advisor in the Education Advisory Service, Auckland College of Education.

Ray Wilson is a Mathematics Advisor in the Education Advisory Service, Auckland College of Education.

Geoff Woolford is a Mathematics Advisor in the Education Advisory Service, Auckland College of Education.

Index

algorithms 122-128, 130
assessment 67, 74, 78-85, 94-108;
    types of 97, 102
behaviourism 36
beliefs 45, 139-149, 165-173
calculators *see* technology
CAN 2,8
collaboration *see* group work
communication 63, 64, 71
computers *see* technology
constructivism 60-76,
content and process 42
context 99, 100, 153
cooperation *see* group work
cooperative skills *see* social and
    cooperative skills
critical mathematics 46,47,172
cultural, issues 150-164; politics
    160, 165
culture 43, 150, 157
curriculum 75, 110-121;
    development 168
discussion *see* communication
formative approach 39
ethnomathematics *see* culture
evaluation 78-85
gender 94-108, 119
group work 21-33, 65
history, of mathematics 171; of
    mathematics education 110-121,
    151
integrating mathematics 40, 153
interactive teaching 28-31, 52, 57,
    73
investigation *see* problem solving
language 159
LOGO 7
Maori 95, 150-153, 157-160, 169
mathematical thinking 50, 52, 56,
    131-133

mathematics, in society 170-171;
    nature of 49, 34-47
new maths 34, 110-121, 151
number algorithms 3
passive learning 71
Piaget 39, 70, 117
planning 78-93
policies and procedures 78-85
politics of mathematics education
    165-174
PrIME 7
problem posing 54
problem solving 4, 41, 62, 73, 99,
    129
process *see* content and process
professional development 118
proof 13-20
questioning 53
reasoning 13-20, 45
refutation 13-20
rich mathematical activities 5, 60-
    62, 74, 86, 90
social and cooperative skills 65
social constructivism 45, 71
structuralism 38, 117
teacher, dilemmas 23; role 5, 9, 22,
    25, 62, 66
technology 2-12, 122-128
thematic approaches 89
Vygotski 45